FEMALE INFANTICIDE
ITS CAUSES AND SOLUTIONS

FEMALE INFANTICIDE
ITS CAUSES AND SOLUTIONS

By

R. Muthulakshmi
Assistant Director
Continuing Education & Extension
~ai Kamaraj University
.mil Nadu
(INDIA)

DISCOVERY PUBLISHING HOUSE PVT. LTD.
NEW DELHI-110 002

First Published-1997
Reprinted-2011

ISBN 81-7141-383-8

Published by
DISCOVERY PUBLISHING HOUSE PVT. LTD.
4383/4A, Ansari Road, Darya Ganj
New Delhi-110 002 (India)
Phone: +91-11-23279245, 43596064-65
Fax: +91-11-23253475
E-mail: parul.wasan@gmail.com
discoverypublishinghouse@gmail.com
web: www.discoverypublishinggroup.com

Printed at:
Dynamic Printers
Delhi

DEDICATED

TO

THE GIRL CHILDREN OF

USILAMPATTI, MADURAI DISTRICT, TAMILNADU

Contents

Foreword

The position of women in the Indian society remains a confused and pathetic one. On the one hand she is glorified as Sakthi and on the other she is looked down upon as a creature born to serve men. As a victim of male domination she does not know where she fits in. Different communities and caste groups and different religious sects have varying attitudes towards women depending on their traditional cultures. In Hinduism, different caste groups treat women differently and most of them treat women as secondary partners in the social frame-work.

In such context, a women faces many problems. Often she is treated as a commodity where she is labelled and priced. This is not a new phenomenon as this can be seen in many countries. In India though attempts are made to correct this through social reforms, new problems are emerging in different magnitudes periodically. The harassment of women has been taking place in different ways as position is still subservient to that of men.

Female infanticide is an extreme form of harrassment towards women and to her society and community. It is a cruel way of getting rid of the female infant soon after birth for no fault of its own. This horrible practice is not only an insult to the new-born child and its mother but also to all women. It is not a problem of any one community but a problem of the entire society, demanding quick solutions.

It is this problem which is analysed in depth in this work. Dr. R. Muthulakshmi who has authored the present book is well-versed in the problem as she had been working in the area where female infanticide has been significant during the past decade. She had tried to educate the women of that area through adult education programmes and during this process she had studied the problem of female infanticide in all its depth.

Dr. R. Muthulakshmi has succeeded in her effort as she was gone deep into the problem using adult education experiments. This work not only gives an elaborate analysis of female infanticide but also explains the experimental method she had used as part of Social Sciences Literature.

I am sure this book will be useful not only to academicians but also to policy makers and all those who are interested in girls' welfare.

Dr. (Mrs.) L. Tharabhai
Prof. of Sociology,
Madurai Kamaraj University

Preface

It was my greatest ambition in life during my college days to work for the welfare of women and children especially for the girls of my community. Suppression of women is a universal fact, but the condition of women in the Kallar Community is such that it has to be studied carefully and sympathetically to get at the true picture.

Piramalai Kallar, a dominant caste is a tribal community which later came to be classified as backward, not only in terms of their culture but also in terms of their status in society. The preservation of the ancient culture has made life difficult for the people of this community especially women. The girls are looked upon as a burden by the community. Women are treated as 'money-bringers' as they have to contribute till their death cash and things to the family they marry into, in order to exist. Many times parents of girl children find it difficult to meet the demands of the community. The problem of dowry increases day by day. At present the demand ranges from Rs. 15,000/- to Lakhs even for an average middle class family. The poorer section of this community also are not exempted from such demands. Thus the girls prove to be a burden economically. In order to escape from such trials the parents of girls opt for eliminating the girls even at birth. In such a context the parents and the elders of the community indulge in female infanticide.

This problem, which is a social menace has to be analysed against the Sociological and Psychological background of the people who form the Community. As hailing from the same background I thought it my duty to find some solutions to this problem and hence this experiment. Most of the people who practise female infanticide are illiterate and hence I have come to believe illiteracy to be the major cause. In order to verify my assumption I used an experimental method of study on the impact of the adult education on such ignorant people utilizing existing theories and rich data available.

I am obliged to many people without whose advise and guidance this work could not have taken the present shape. First and foremost I should place on record the continuous encouragement and thought-provoking directions I received from Dr. (Mrs.) L. Tharabhai, Professor of Sociology, Madurai Kamaraj University, without whose guidance and cooperation, I could not have completed this work.

I am indebted to Prof. R. Rengasamy, who was kind enough to spare me from my department work, whenever I got engrossed in my research. Also Colleagues Mr. G. Ramakrishnan, Mrs. Malini, Dr. A. Muthumanickam, Mr. Venkatakannan and Mr. Athiyaman never shirked to do my part of work whenever I was away. Miss Nirmala Mary, Prof. P. V. Ramachandran gave me a supporting hand in carrying out this venture.

Mr. Thangamuthu typed the thesis.

The most important people who form the core of this work are the women of Usilampatti who were my respondents.

The ICCW of Usilampatti, was of great help to me while I was doing the project. Mr. N.S. Selvan, Anusuyadevi and Dinesh Babu deserve special mention as they helped me in every possible way.

Dr. R. Muthulakshmi

1

Introduction

The family is the basic unit of society. However, the nature and structure of the family change from society to society and also differ within the same society over a period of time. Family is flexible both in structure and function, but the family system is not questioned either by philosophers or academicians. The unit of a family consists of the members of the family, and all the members have the same status in it. Though this is the underlying principle, the status is assigned within the family and each member is differentiated from others by his status. In every family the individual occupies a definite ascribed status. Each family has various status-groups which are hierarchically structured. In the joint family the status-structure is very complex. In includes members belonging to different age, sex and generation categories related either on affined or consanguineous relationship. One of the determining factors of status in the Indian family is sex. The women members of the family get subordinate status due to various factors. In a patriarchal society as in India, the authority of the male is never questioned and hence accepted by all. Usually the authority of the woman depends upon her husband's status and hence he has only a secondary status[1] in the family.

The position of women is not uniform in India. Women had freedom in the ancient society of pre-Vedic and early Vedic times. "Education was not denied to girls who went to Gurukulas or forest universities, studying side by side with boys in co-educational institutions. It was a father's bounden duty to educate his daughters as well as his sons".[2]

During the Vedic period, women and men were treated equally. The Aryan women had complete control over the household and hers was a predominant influence on the children. She even enjoyed the privilege of suyamvara, or choosing the life-partner from many suitors. The Brahmanical literature, the epics and the post-epic literature are replete with instances illustrating bridal choice. The wedding hymn narrates the marriage of Surya, the Sun-maiden with Soma, attesting the divine origin of the institution of marriage.[3] The hymn metaphorically describes the bride and the groom, in terms of rituals, formulas and sayings. The marriage becomes a visible reality when the parents give the bribe their farewell blessings.

On arrival at her new home, the bride is welcomed with wishes of wealth and progeny, soliciting her watchful care of the house. "Here (home) may be the delight through wealth and progeny. Give this house thy watchful care. Live with thy husband in old age; may you still rule your household".[4] As they proceed with the wedding hymn, it is the husband who pronounces the final benediction by wishing her happiness through the grace of the Indra and her installation to rule over this household. Thus one can see that woman, whether she was daughter, wife or mother, had absolute supremacy during the time of the Vedas.

The position of women slowly underwent certain changes as they started confining themselves to the household. In the later Vedic period, woman became more a bridal figure than a feminine figure. During this time women were considered submissive human beings and not equal partners. Epics have assigned a different role to women. The women in the Ramayana and the Mahabharatha played crucial roles in the politics and economy of their played crucial roles in the politics and economy of their countries but they were not given a supreme position at any time. Sita, Draupadi, Gandhari and Kunthi prove women's secondary role. In the Buddhist period the lot of women did not improve over what it was in the epic period. Though Buddha considered men and women equal for reaping the fruits of Karma, he believed that particularly a woman had to depend upon her own acts for her future salvation. This principle enhanced the status of women during the Buddhist period.

In the Hindu literature, women's position seems to be fluctuating. In the early Sanskrit literature women are depicted as showing their valour and administrative capacity. Megasthanese, in his famous book, *Indica*, wrote of the women; some sat on chariots, some on horses and some even on elephants and they were equipped with weapons of every kind as if they were going on "campaigns". Kautilya assigned a very low position he wrote the Arthasastra. He holds that the maintenance of wife and children is the responsibility of the husband, and Kautilya did not recommend women for the duties of state, though the mentioned here and there that women could be used as spies or bodyguards.

In order to understand the position of women in the Hindu society, one should know how women had been portrayed in it. In Hinduism the concept of female has a dual role. "On the one hand, woman is fertile, benevolent — the bestower; on the other she is aggressive, malevolent, the destroyer."[6] These two facets of "femaleness" are culturally acknowledged. The female is regarded as Prakriti by nature.[7] Understanding Hindu women is possible also by understanding the rules and the models laid down in the Hindu society. A cultural theme of the norm and guidelines says that woman should be under the control of man and her power should always be subordinate to that of man. The most dominant role for the Hindu woman is the role as wife. Many classical Hindu laws focus on this. The basic role of woman according to the laws of Manu is as follows:

"By a young girl, by a young woman or even by an aged one, nothing must be done independently even in her own house.

In childhood a female must be subject to her father, in youth to her husband, when her lord is dead to her sons; a woman must never be independent."[8]

"Though destitute of virtue, or seeing pleasure (elsewhere) or devoid of good qualities (yet) a husband must be constantly worshipped as a god by a faithful wife.

By violating her duty towards her husband a wife is disgraced in this world: (after death). She enters the womb of a Jackal, and is tormented by diseases (the punishment) of her sin.

She who controls her thoughts, words and deeds never slights her lord, resides (after death) with her husband (in heaven) and is called a virtuous (wife).

Day and night, woman must be kept in dependency by the males (of) their (families) and if they attach themselves to sensual enjoyments they must be kept under one's control considering that the highest duty of all castes, Even weak husband (must) strive to guard their wives.

Women did not care for beauty, nor is their attention fixed on age (thinking) (It is enough that) he is a man", they give themselves to the handsome and ugly.

Through their passion for men, through their mutable temper, through their natural heartlessness, they become disloyal towards their husbands, however carefully they are guarded in this (world).

Knowing their disposition which the Lord of creatures laid in them at the creation to be such, (every) man should most strenuously exert himself to guard them."[9]

These ideas on women are not peculiar to Sanskrit literature and but can also be seen in the vernacular writings. They appear and reappear very often emphasising that the laws of Manu have become customs of society. These customs were later changed into values. Women's position in society was more or less fixed. From this period onwards women got only a submissive, secondary, dependent role and men became supreme. Though she gets respect, the mother is always dependent on her father, husband on grown-up sons. The wife, whose is the most important role in Hinduism, is full of subordination, devotion and duty. The daughter obeys her father, and the sister is under the protection of her brother.

Though scholars, philosophers and administrators have tried to change the position of women, it has been very difficult because Hinduism which is the root of Indian society has firmly laid down the position of Indian women. Though many foreign invasions were witnessed in India, women's position remained unchanged. There was a change in the society when the British ruled India. The British rule made an impact on the economic, educational, political and industrial segments of India which in turn affected the social structure of the country. Values like liberty, equality, respect for the individual, and secularism, were, introduced in colonial India which had repercussions in the various sections of life.

During this period India saw two great movements, namely, social reform movement and Independence movement which affected the status of the individual and the groups. Both these movements questioned the status of women.

The social reform movement is regarded as a key to the intellectual process that went into the making of modern India. The issues which attracted the attention of the nineteenth century social reformers were sati, the ill-treatment of widows, the misery of the widows, denial of property rights, and education of women. Social reformers felt that these social evils should be eradicated by raising the awareness of the people and making them sensitive to the injustice perpetuated on women.

As the social reform movement, the national movement also changed the attitude of women considerably. "Women organised themselves into groups and were willing to join processions, face police firing and even go to prison. They broke the salt law, picketed shops which sold liquor and foreign-manufactured cloth. There were women who joined terrorist groups and helped in editing and distributing banned newspapers and in manufacturing bombs"[10]. While evaluating the Gujarati women's response to Gandhi's call during 1920-1942, Aparna Basu comments that it was an impressive record.[11] She remarks, "women indulged in various kinds of activities ranging from mass scale popular agitations, constructive work among Harijans and Adivasis, to formal institutionalised electoral politics."[12] Thus one can see that during the Independence movement an awareness was created in the society to remove the social disability of women. Education was given to them to a certain extend and women slowly started emerging out of the house. Women of contemporary India still struggle with various problems. Women of all classes and religions and women in different walks of life face problems. By and large women in the cities, towns, and villages remain the same with a lot of problems in the long course of their lives.

Women's Problems in India

The problems of women are many in number and mostly all the problems of society are considered to be women's problems. In a patriarchal society like that of India, the society is structured and made to functioi as man wants it to and not as the female wishes it to be. Woman': psychology is not understood by the society and hence she is alway required to adjust to the needs of men. In this process women face man problems from their birth to death.

Women is often looked down upon as a course on the society. For all its problems the society finds fault with women since they are the weaker sex. Woman is kept aloof from the opposite sex resulting in separation, restriction and confinement. She is often seen only as child producing machine, yet if she gives birth to a female child, the society does not respect her.

Social degradation of women was taken advantage of by men, and women were treated on par with domestic animals. Women were given no property rights and hence women became a burden to the father or the brother. Gifts brought by the bribe were important than the bribe herself. Dowry, one of the evils, came into existence when society looked upon woman more as a burden. The presence of girls in the family was seen as an economic calamity in the family. Most of these problems of women which started from the latter Vedic period continue even to the present-day society. These problems have accumulated.

Infanticide— Woman's Problem

Most of the problems of society are the problems of women. By and large men have a tendency to escape the problems whereas women are subjected to the problems. Thus illiteracy, dowry, crime, poverty etc., are more problematic to women than to men. If a crime is committed by an individual, the wife, the mother and the daughter of the offender are affected psychologically more than the criminal himself. Dowry is another case in point. Infanticide is also not an exception to this. Female children are very often the victims of infanticide.

The act of killing the female child is not a unitary phenomenon as it has several dimensions such as economic, political, social and psychological. Therefore, the phenomenon of female infanticide is to be treated or analysed as a complex problem. The problem is complex because it affects not only the child's mother but also the family and society at large.

To make it more specific, one can say that female infanticide is the act of killing the new born girl within 24 to 48 hours of birth.[13] Female infanticide is different from infant mortality. Infant mortality is natural death whereas the former is murder.

Female infanticide started in India as human sacrifice. Infanticide was prevalent in India from the early 19th century. According to Jacob

Bryant, "One would think it scarcely possible that so unnatural a custom as that of human sacrifices could have existed in the world, but it is very certain that it is not only existed, but almost universally prevailed".[14] Bryant says human sacrifice was prevalent among the Egyptians. The Arabs also used to practice infanticide as sacrifice.

Historical View of Female infanticide

The people of Duma in particular sacrificed every year a child, and buried it beneath an altar, which they worshipped as they did not worship images. The Persians buried people alive. Amestris, the wife of Xerxes, entombed twelve persons alive, for the good of her soul. It would be endless to endless to enumerate every city, or every province, where these practice prevailed. The Cyprians, the Rhodians, the Pheonicians, those of Chios, Lesbos, Tenedos, all prescribed human sacrifices.[15] The Romans were also accustomed to this type of practice. These practices prevailed among all the people of northern Europe. The Massageta, the Scythians, the Getes, the Sarmatians all the various nations beyond the Baltic, particularly the Suevi and Scandinavians, held it as a fixed principle that their happiness and security could be obtained only at the expense of the lives of others. This customs prevailed in Great Mexico and most parts of America. In Africa the people sacrificed some of the captives taken in war to their fetiches in order to secure their favour.

People of many religions practiced human sacrifice at some time or the other. Among the Hindus, the act of human sacrifice was practised in different ways. The human sacrifice among the Hindus goes back to the early 5th century and till date one see the custom prevailing among the Hindus. The Muslims of Arabia also practised human sacrifice. For Example, the Pagan Arabs buried their daughters alive. Though we can find infanticide in various forms and ways in different countries most of the countries stopped this custom by the middle or the late 19th century. However, in certain countries like India infanticide still revails.

Infanticide in India

In India female infanticide prevailed before and after 19th century. It was the British Government which took the initiative to stop this custom. In India the custom of female infanticide originated as a sacrifice to God in some part of Bengal. In some parts of Orissa when the couple had no children for a long time they took a vow to the Goddess Ganga, that, if she bestowed them with children they would offer the firstborn to her. If they were blessed with children the eldest was reared for three or four years and on an auspicious day it was given a holy bath in the river; the child was encouraged to go farther and farther into the water till it was carried away by the stream. This kind of offering is still practised in some parts of Orissa.[16]

The principal places in Bengal where this kind of murder is practised are Ganga, Saugur, Calcutta, Trivenee, Nudeeya, Chakdhuh, and Prayag or Allahabad. Infanticide is practised in several ways. If an infant refuses the mother's breast, it is considered to be under the influence of some malignant spirit. Such a child is put into a basket, and hung up in a tree where the evil spirit is supposed to reside. That child is generally destroyed by ants, of birds or prey: but sometimes it perishes by neglect.

In the North-Western parts of Hindustan, the horrid practice of sacrificing female children as soon as they are born has been known from time immemorial. Amongst the Rajputs female infanticide was more common. The reason attributed was that there was a custom of hypergamy whereby they cannot get their daughters married to the lower caste bridegrooms. They had to find husbands for their daughters in caste groups of equal rank or higher status. This was very costly as high caste-bride-groom demanded heavy dowry.

The birth of a daughter is considered a humiliating event, and rarely it is a subject for congratulations; while the birth of a son is celebrated with great ostentation and hilarity. At the same time the crime of female murder is a grave offence according to the Hindu shastras:

To kill one Brahmun is equal to killing one hundred cows;

To kill one woman is equal to killing one hundred Brahmuns;

To kill one child is equal to killing one hundred women;

To kill one hundred children is an offence too heinous for comparison.[17]

This contradictory picture of women is found throughout the Hindu scriptures. On the one hand women are worshipped and on the other hand they are viewed as forms of evil.

During the nineteenth century female infanticide was prevalent among the Rajputs. It was also seen in Bengal. Later it spread to the states like Orissa, Gujarat etc. From the later pat of the nineteenth century efforts were taken to reduce female infanticide and human sacrifice. The British Government and many social reformers took the lead for the abolition of female infanticide. Several legislations were passed by the British Government.

There was strong resistance in the initial stage to the abolition of infanticide. Along with female infanticide other practices like sathi, widow remarriage and other restrictions on women were also suspended. In the beginning of the nineteenth century strict legislations were made.[18] The independent India was by and large free from female infanticide. But during the recent period when the economic conditions became very poor when there is a imbalance between economic conditions and social conditions people started various inhuman activities. This is because the social values were more emotional and dear to the people, than the economic conditions if one is looking the following Table 1.1 one can understand the condition of women in India.

Table 1.1 : Education and Employment Status of Women

Sl. No.	*States*	*Female Literacy (%)*	*Female Employment (%)*
1.	Rajasthan	20.84	13.34
2.	Madhya Pradesh	28.39	23.08
3.	Bihar	23.10	10.04
4.	Tamil Nadu	52.29	26.31

Source : India 1991, Research and Reference Division, Ministry of Information and Broadcasting, Government of India

The women do not educational, economic and political status and therefore women are considered a burden to the society. Child marriages and dowry are common features here. Polygamy is also practised to a certain extent. The female child is not treated properly and its birth itself is considered a sad affair.

Infanticide in Tamil Nadu

In Tamil Nadu female infanticide is a recent phenomenon when compared with other states. Female infanticide was a vogue in ancient times in Tamil Nadu but later it disappeared only to reappear in 1960 in certain pockets. Female infanticide is an economic phenomenon among certain castes in certain regions in Tamil Nadu. The problem of dowry and other financial problem related to a girl's marriage forced the killing of female babies at the time of birth itself. These problems are acute among Kallar women in Usilampatti, Kullathoor village in Salem district and Valliankadu village in Periyar district.[19] Kallars are predominantly seen in the Usilampatti taluk of Tamil Nadu. The community is most backward and therefore killing a female child has been a social phenomenon among them. It is reported that female infanticide has been practised among the Kallars during the past twenty years. The prime cause for female infanticide is the lower economic status of Kallars. This is widely practised among the lower income groups of the community.

Female children are killed in this community by several means. Some of them are killed immediately after their birth. In the case of a hospital delivery the female child disappears even without the knowledge of hospital authorities. This phenomenon which started in the early sixties is now spread throughout the district of Madurai where the community is concentrated. Therefore one can infer that a phenomenon becomes a social phenomenon when the practices are accepted by the communities. It also becomes the culture of the community. This practice also resulted in the negative proportion of male-female ratio. Formerly women were more among the Kallars, whereas men outnumber women now.

Dimensions of Female Infanticide

Education and Female Infanticide

Modernisation is possible through education. In a society where economic condition is poor, education is the primary means of social change. Improvement of society and liberation of women are possible only if the people are properly educated; education should be given primary importance as a tool of social change.

Female Infanticide and Economic Factors

Not only education but also economic, political and social factors are related to the practice of female infanticide. Infanticide is largely found among poor people. The middle class and upper class sections do not generally practice infanticide. People who do not have means of living find it difficult to spend money for religious and social functions. As the society is caste-bound even those who come from poor income groups have to obey the rules and regulations of the caste. The expenses in connection with earboring, puberty ceremonies, pregnancy and child birth are very heavy. The daughters make their parents slaves to somebody else through borrowing. These reasons force the parents to think of female infanticide.

Political and Social causes of Female Infanticide

Political and social causes have a relationship with Female Infanticide. Recently the female infanticide practiced in the district of Madurai attracted the attention of the Government. As a result the district now is provided with small scale Industries units, adult education centres, infant care centres both private and public.

Social factors related to female infanticide are many when compared with the economic and educational factors. The customs prevailing in the area are such that there is a clear discrimination between the male and the female. The male is considered a source of economic gain. The female is considered a burden to the society. It is interesting to note that among the Kallars of Usilampatti a girl becomes a property for the maternal uncles and cross-cousins. Such Kinsmen have a right to marry the girl. In order to escape this evil custom, parents consider femal infanticide an easy solution. Other social factors are linked with economic factors like marriage and child-birth, to name a few. Therefore, one can say that socio-economic and religious factors are interrelated and all these factors operate together in female infanticide. Thus, it is not a single cause phenomenon, but a multidimensional one.

Features of Infanticide in Tamil Nadu

It is found that female infanticide has not been mentioned in any of the literature of ancient times. So the phenomenon of female infanticide is a recent one which has a social and economic base.

Kallars belong to the community of "Thevar" or "Mukkulathor" which comprises three divisions such as Kallars, Maravars and Agamudayars. The meaning of "Thevar" literally means celestial beings or divine-natured people and "Mukkulathor" means three clans united together. People believed that these three clans descended from three ancient major clans namely Cholas (Kallars), Pandians (Maravars) and Cheras (Agamudairs). It is said that Indira had a sexual relationship with a celestial female, out of which were born Kallan, Maravan and Agamudaian.[20]

From the very early days that is from the Sangam period, the terms "Kallan" and "Maravan" were used but only from the sixteenth century these communities were identified. All the communities live in the southern districts of Tamil Nadu, namely. Tiruchirappalli, Thanjavur, Tirunelveli, Madurai, Ramanathapuram, Kamarajar and Pasumpon Thevar. Kallars are found mainly in Thanjavur, Madurai, Pudukkottai and Tiruchirappalli.[21] These communities are endogamous in nature. Each community believes that it is superior to the other, though historically all the three have no major differences. Each community has sub-sects which are endogamous in nature.

The Kallars are very hard-working and their traditional occupation is agriculture. They are known for their criminal activity. The Government of Tamil Nadu designated them as Denotified Tribe, till 1992.

The women of Kallar community are extraordinarily clever and they supervise household work in the absence of men. The entire household responsibility is given to kallar women. Kallar women are known for their bravery also. There is a wide belief that it is this bravery which has given them the courage to kill their own babies. Thus caste and female infanticide are closely associated. It can be seen that female infanticide is prevalent in some areas of Tamil Nadu where this caste is present.

Another peculiar characteristic is the regional relationship of this phenomenon. The region in which the Kallars are in the majority, is economically backward. The area being rural is totally cut off from the urban area and the standard of living is very low. Women and children are kept outside the mainstream. Education is not given to them. Since no employment and economic activities are provided for these groups, their life is pathetic. The region is poverty-stricken. The educated people of this region migrate to other parts of the State in search of employment leaving the illiterate and the poor in the area. The tradition-bound region has no other go but to condemn them to a life of poverty.

The social and economic conditions along with the backwardness in education create a suitable condition for female infanticide. One can attribute all these factors to the root cause, poverty. If poverty is eradicated through economic modernisation via education, one can hope to curb this cruel evil. Therefore, the problem under investigation is considered a multi-dimensional one and a major solution for the eradication of the problem can be achieved through education.

Objectives of the Study

Female infanticide which started in the ancient days are again seen recently in certain areas of Tamil Nadu, Rajasthan, Bihar etc. In Tamil Nadu the phenomenon of female infanticide is region-specific and caste-specific in nature. Considering these two aspects the present study concentrates on the regions where the caste which indulges in female infanticide is in majority.

In the central part of Tamil Nadu in Madurai where Thevars are in majority female infanticide is very common. This study aims to analyse female infanticide in this community. The community is concentrated in and around Madurai, especially in Usilampatti taluk. Usilampatti area has been selected for a detailed study of female infanticide.

Two villages have been selected making one an experimental village and the other a control village. The two villages are far apart and one village cannot influence the other.

As the female infanticide has been practised for the past 20 years, an attempt is made to study only the existing pattern of the phenomenon. The first objective is:

1) To study the pattern of female infanticide in two select villages.

In order to reduce female infanticide a change in attitude is necessary, and therefore the second objective is—

2) Changing the attitude of women with special reference to female infanticide.

This study tries to change the attitude through an external stimulus, namely education; therefore the next objective is—

3) To study the impact of adult education on the rate of female infanticide.

Changing the attitude is not the end. The main goal of this study is to eliminate female infanticide. In order to achieve this, one should know the various ways and means of reducing the rate of female infanticide.

In order to achieve the objectives mentioned above the following objective is also to be met.

4) Evolving an adult education kit which can be used in those areas where the female infanticide is practised.

5) Evolving other educational tools like video films, adult education primer and audio cassettes.

Methodology of the Study

Area of the Study

Madurai district lies in the south of Tamil Nadu. The district of Madurai is divided into nine taluks and one of the taluks is Usilampatti. Usilampatti lies 40 Km. west of Madurai. Its population is 276, 201 (8.01%).[22] This dry region is predominantly an agricultural region depending mainly on rain fall. Paddy, cotton, ground nuts, cholam, kampu and ragi are the main crops in Usilampatti area.

Because of the dryness, the area is also having very low humidity and agriculture is also seasonal. The economy of the area depends very much upon this factor. Therefore, the employment opportunities are meagre. Migration of population both permanent and seasonal is common. Usilampatti taluk constitutes 92 villages consisting of 276, 201 (8.01%) population.[23] There is a small town (Usilampatti) in the Taluk.

As the area does not have much forest the people find it difficult to manage the fuel for day to day living. The literacy level of the area is

Table 1.2 : The Male and Female Population in the Taluk

Category	*Male*	*Female*	*Total*
Rural	128,307 (46.45%)	121,506 (44%)	249,813 (90.45%)
Urban	13,624 (4.93%)	12,764 (4.62%)	26,388 (9.55%)
Overall	141,931 (51.38%)	134,270 (48.62%)	276,201 (100%)

Source : 1991 Census Publication (Provisional Population Totals)

Table 1.3 : Land Use Pattern

Sl. No.	Land Utilisation	Area in Hectares during 1990-91 Census	Area in Ha No. during 1960-61 Census
1.	Forest	17,232	18,332
2.	Barren and Uncultivable	24,314	23,165
3.	Current follows	16,392	13,421
4.	Net area sown	23,029	23,156
5.	Total Cropped Area	23,423	25,937

Source : 1991 Census Publication (Provisional Population Totals).

44.82%. There are 172 primary schools, 30 middle schools, 12 high schools, 4 higher secondary schools, 2 colleges and 3 teacher colleges in the taluk.

Though educational institutions are many in number, the literates are only 44.82. The literacy rate in Usilampatti taluk has been compared, in the following table, with the literacy rates in the district and State levels.

Table 1.4 : Literacy Level

(Figures in Percentage)

Year	State	District	Taluk
1961	36.57	38.41	26.74
1971	42.65	43.23	29.82
1981	46.76	47.36	34.00
1991	63.72	53.25	44.82

Source : Census of India. Tamil Nadu. Series 19. Part IX.

As compared with the State literacy rate and the district literacy rate, the Usilampatti rate is low.

In Usilampati taluk, the literacy rate among males is higher when compared with that of the female. Most of the children are not sent to school.

Land-holding population is very small in this region. Though most people are engaged in cultivation.

The standard of living is average and 43.26% of houses are living

Table 1.5 : Male Female Literacy Rate in Usilampatti Taluk

(Figures in Percentage)

Year	*Male*	*Female*
1961	36.20	16.17
1971	40.41	17.91
1981	46.25	21.82
1991	56.48	32.51

Source : 1961 Census of India, Tamil Nadu, Series 19, Part IX.

below the poverty line. Even the essential items like rice, wheat, vegetables, pulses and oil and costly and luxury for the people.

Sample of the Study

A sample of two villages has been selected for intensive study. A pilot study in this area revealed the occurrence of female infanticide more in certain area. It was decided to take two villages which have higher frequencies of female infanticide. One village is kept under control and the other is used as an experimental village. The study used an experimental design to test the impact of adult education for reducing the rate of female infanticide.

Though only two village are selected for the study, the case studies cover the entire district.

The villages selected for the purpose of investigation are Nadumuthalikkulam and Kuppanampatti. The former is the experimental village and latter is the control village. For the purpose of case studies all the incidents occuring the district were taken. All the females in the villages who were between 15-35 years are taken for attitude study. The village have been selected on the basis of frequency of female infanticide.

Unit of the Study

There are two units for this study, the first unit being the households in which female infanticide occurs and the second unit of the study being the female population between 15-35 years.

Tools and Techniques for the Study

For the purpose of caste study, interviews were conducted with the help of tape recorders. Observation was also one of the major techniques because the study needs a careful understanding of the peoples' attitude, motivation etc. The main tool of the study was the preparation of the adult education supplementary reader. This was done after making a thorough analysis of the village. The village was studied with the help of interview-schedules and the analysis was done on the basis of secondary data such as video cassettes, tape recorders and interviews with the old people. Four adult education centres were organised for the study, two in the experimental village and two in the control village.

The adult education Primer included short stories, role play, dialogue, conversation and lecture series, Audio cassettes were played to the people at different periods in the experimental village. This was done through the adult education centres.

References

1. Here "secondary status" is used to denote the women's status becuase women's superior position in the family in India is not considered as inevitable.
2. Mayah Balse, *The Indian Female Attitude Towards Sex*, p.13.
3. Zanaide A. Ragozin, *Vedic India*, p. 368.
4. The Wedding Hymn in *Rigveda* : X as quoted in Tripat Sharma, *Women in Ancient India* (from 320 A.D. to c. 1200 A.D.), p.9.
5. J.W.M. Crindle (Tr.) *Magasthenese Fragments*, XXVII.
6. Jacobson Doranne and Susans Wadley, *Women in India : Two Perspectives*, 1986, p. 114.
7. *Ibid.*, p. 115.
8. *Ibid.*, p. 121.
9. *Ibid.*
10. Neera Desai and Maithreyi Krishnaraj, *Women and Society in India*, 1987, p. 40.
11. *Ibid.*
12. *Ibid.*

13. Ibid.
14. *J. Peggs, Cries of Agony; An Historical Account of Suttee, Infanticide, Ghat Murder and Slavery in India*, p. 131.
15. *Ibid.*
16. *Ibid.*, p. 131.
17. *Ibid.*, p. 143.
18. B.V. Gupta, *Revolution and Status of Women in India*, 1982, p. 51.
19. "Penn Kulanthaigal Piranthathum Kolai", *Junior Viketan* (T), November 1990, pp. 4–5.
20. K. Bose, *Forward Block : A Sociological Profile of Mukkulathors*, 1988, p. 49.
21. *Ibid.*, p. 50.
22. *Census of India 1991*, p. 75
23. *Ibid.*

2

Female Infanticide—A Review in the Villages

Introduction

Female infanticide is an indicator of women's position in India. Women are considered a burden to the society due to several factors. Therefore, they are not even given a chance to live and come up in society. As soon as a female baby is born she is immediately killed so that she and others can escape the problems of life. The baby girls are killed because the condition of women existing in the society is so deplorable that a girl has to suffer from birth to death.

Generally female infanticide is considered a symptom of fear in the society. From the opinions available regarding female infanticide, two different facts emerge. On the issue of female infanticide one school of thought considers female infanticide as prevailing in the communities where women are considered a burden and treated inferior in the society. Therefore the women indulge in female infanticide as a protest against their own suffering. The second school of thought, considered as a modern view, holds that the customs and traditions of the society are so rigid, the people are afraid of them and are in fear of advocating change.

According to the traditional view female infanticide is considered a general pattern in the community which has now become part of the customs. It is to be noted that this custom has spread throughout the State, wherever the Piramalaikallar live. One can say that the practice of infanticide is one among the several rituals prevalent in the community. The people of this community are now very much familiar with this custom that nobody considers it as a "surprise" phenomenon.

When this is the traditional view, the contemporary view considers that female infanticide as a negative social approach. This school is of the opinion that female infanticide has to be abolished either through education or through economy or by any other mode. Here female infanticide is considered a curse of the community.

Though there is no proper definition of female infanticide one can say that female infanticide is the practice of killing the female baby immediately after birth by resorting to such practices and techniques such as deliberate delay in feeding, non-feeding, less feeding etc.[1]

While killing of female babies is resorted to by the rural people, in the cities female fetus is aborted after determining the sex through scientific tests. One of the recent studies shows that between 1978 and 1983 as many as 78 thousand female babies were aborted after the gender was determined through various clinical tests.[2]

In the cities of Tamil Nadu there are many clinical laboratories, to determine the sex of the baby before birth. Whereas villages like Usilampatti have no such facilities. In the villages of Tamil Nadu such as Usilampatti one can see the conceived mother praying to God: "I don't want a female baby, please bless me with a male child." We find some mothers of female babies christening their babies as Pothum Ponnu, Pothumadi and Pothumani.[3] There are different forms of vows and prayers offered to God for begetting a male child.

If prayers do not bless them with a male child they indulge in female infanticide. Therefore, one can say that female infanticide is not only socially motivated but there are many other factors which motivate people to kill their female babies.

General Causes of Female Infanticide

The causes of female infanticide in the area, where the study was conducted, can be mainly classified as economic and social causes. Though there are certain other motivating factors they can be included in any one of these two categories. The female infanticide is practiced by the lower class people and therefore it is considered mainly as an economic phenomenon. Most of them find it hard to have one square meal a day, it is also found that the people who are unemployed or underemployed kill the girl child after its birth.

The female child is killed not only because they cannot bring the baby up but also they are afraid that they have to meet heavy expenses for ceremonies connected with the girl child, such as the marriage ceremony, earboring ceremony and puberty ceremony. All people irrespective of their economic background have to celebrate these ceremonies. The marriage ceremony is the most expensive ceremony in the community. Dowry is one of the major demands in this community, and the marriage is fixed only after satisfactory dowry negotiations. Dowry includes money for the entire expenditure connected with the marriage ceremony and jewels for the bride and some gifts for the bridegroom such as gold chain, gold ring and in some cases houses, car etc. After the marriage bride and the groom are invited to the bride's family with some gifts. This is called *maruveedu*. After this, for all religious festivals and village festivals, the bride and the bridegroom have to be invited by the bride's family, which involves a heavy expenditure. The birth ceremony is another costly ceremony. The community believes that unless the rituals are performed both the child and the mother will be affected. Therefore ceremonies like announcement of pregnancy, *valaikappu*, and *Marunthukkali* are celebrated. After the delivery also the expenditure increases. The bride's parents have to take care of the delivery and after the delivery, child and mother have to be given gold jewels, new clothes and money. The next important ceremony is the earboring ceremony. This is done for the female as well as for the male child and the expenditure is again met by mother's parents. After this, puberty ceremony is also celebrated by the girl's grandparents and maternal uncles. This ceremony extends for seven days. The maternal uncle will feed all the relatives and present the gold chain and new clothes to the girl. The last is the death ceremony which also involves expenditure. Here again the women's parents have to meet all the expenses.

From the above analysis one can understand the expenditure involved during the life of a girl, apart from the day-to-day expenditure on her maintenance, education etc.

Many people borrow money to fulfil these social commitments. The spending pattern of this community is also so extravagant that there is no relationship between income and expenditure. Regular drought and failure of monsoon weaken the economic background of this community. Such bad socio-economic conditions account for illiteracy and ignorance. The female children are very rarely sent to school which again blocks their way in getting a decent job. Industrially also the area is backward which again in gives very little scope for the improvement of the income.

Social Cause of Female Infanticide

The social causes lead to economic problems. Apart from the social causes which have been mentioned earlier there are some others also. According to C. Kubendran and S. Gurusamy the four social factors which motivate female infanticide are

i) Desire to avoid unwanted female babies,

ii) Escape from illegitimacy,

iii) Desire to limit the family size and

iv) Fear of deformity or sickness in the child.[4]

As the female babies are not respected by the society, there is a tendency even among the middle class parents to avoid female babies. As per their belief the prestige of the community lies in the male child. The parent will try for a male child and if their attempts fail their immediate task is to take the extreme step of killing the babies. This tendency is seen among many couples of Usilampatti area.

Another social factor which influences female infanticide is illegitimate pregnancy. There is a custom in the community of preferential marriages. Preferential marriages are accepted as legitimate by the society. The cross-cousins and maternal uncles have a "property right" over their cross-cousins or nieces. Cousins will not be questioned if they have a sexual relationship with their preferential cousins or nieces. It is understood that the girls by and large do not like such relationship but the boys prefer it. The consequence is that the parents of the girls wish to give their daughters to some boys from outside. In the mean time, if girl conceives, the parents of the girls try to hide the pregnancy or kill the child. Among the poor sections of the community the illegitimate pregnancy leads to female infanticide, because the girls will not marry for economic reasons.

Desire to limit the family is another cause of female infanticide. The family planning methods rarely reach the community. The modern methods of contraception are not available in the area and therefore often women are not able to avoid pregnancy. They realise the danger of having a big family. The fear of abortion coupled with the desire for a male child leads to the delivery of the child. If the family is oversized and the baby born is female, there is a tendency to kill the child to reduce the size of the family.

Psychological causes also lead to female infanticide. If the child born is deformed or found to have some sickness, the parents do not mind killing the child. The philosophy behind this is to avoid its suffering throughout its life. The causes of female infanticide so far analysed are the community causes found in the Usilampatti area. Religion also sometimes provides the cause. The female babies are sacrificed to Gods in certain parts of the community, as religious offerings, which is not done by the Piramalaikallars. The community believes that religion permits the killing of the female child instead of making it suffer through life. Though there is no religious authority supporting female infanticide, the people of former generations gave a religious colour to such acts by framing songs, stories, and folk-lore in support of female infanticide.

Female Infanticide and the Immediate Society

Female infanticide is a problem for the community, for the family and for the individuals who commit this act. Though it is practised by Piramalaikallars, it is viewed as a social problem because it down-grades the human beings especially the females. Therefore, it is to be viewed as a social problem. Female infanticide is considered by sociologists as a humiliation to women. Applying the Marxian Theory of alienation, female infanticide is an extreme manifestation of the feeling of alienation, from the point of view of the parents. The parents feel that the child and the mother will be alienated from the society if she does not kill her child. Therefore, the mother resorts to killing the child. Here the alienation is caused by the society. The responsibility of female infanticide should therefore be shouldered by the society itself.

Though the Piramalaikallars are the community which practises female infanticide, the other communities in the area are also affected by the act. People of other communities are afraid that the act will spread to their communities.

Just like the society, the females concerned are also affected by the female infanticide. They are affected sociologically as well as psychologically. Sociologically the female infanticide creates feelings towards parents and social acceptance from the other sections of the community. Though majority of community people are indifferent towards the act., atleast a few of them criticize female infanticide. It is this attitude which gives the society the acceptance for this social phenomenon. The individuals who are around the family also are affected by female infanticide. The parents are affected immediately. Here it is interesting to note that even the parents want to refrain from killing the baby. People around them, particularly parents of the pregnant lady, her husband and other relatives explain the consequences of delivering a girl child. This is a form of anticipatory socialization whereby the conceived women will be preparing herself to kill the child if the baby whom the society or the community considers as unwanted. It is not only the parents who are affected by the act of female infanticide but also other family members like siblings, grandparents etc. The siblings are especially affected because they are future mothers and fathers. They see the act of female infanticide and this they adopt in their life too. Thus the society, family and the individual are affected by the female infanticide in different degrees.

The following case studies reveal the motivation, causes and the process of female infanticide, usually occurring in the study area.

Case Study—I

In the village of Ampattayanpatti, a case of female infanticide was identified between 1985-1990. The exact date of killing the girl child is not known.

The village is an agricultural village but only a few families own lands and the rest are only agricultural labourers. Paddy and ground-nut are the chief crops though here and there vegetables are cultivated.

Mokkasamy Thevar and Thangammal, are a couple among the agricultural labourers. Though they were poverty-stricken they were happy. They gave birth to a female child whom they named as Meenakshi. Meenakshi was brought up in accordance with the capacity of her parents and she grew up into a matured and healthy girl. Meenakshi was given in marriage to her own maternal uncle. The parents were happy. The marriage took place in Meenakshi's house and later Meenakshi and Rasu, her husband moved in to their house. Neither Meenakshi nor Rasu owned any property and therefore both of them worked as agricultural labourers. They were living a happy family life till she conceived for the first time. The family was looking forward for a male child from Meenakshi but unfortunately the first issue was a female child. The baby girl was looked after well. The parents believed that the girl would bring prosperity to the family.

Soon Meenakshi became pregnant again. As soon as she became pregnant people around her spread a story that she would suffer a lot if she gave birth to a female child.

Meenakshi prayed to all the Gods for a male child. The relatives of Meenakshi were also anxious. Unfortunately the second baby also was a female. So they decided to do away with the child. Immediately after delivery the child was killed in the presence of the mother. They put rose petals into the throat of the baby which made the baby suffocate and die.

The mother of the baby took atleast two days to recover from the shock. Though the relatives consoled her, Meenakshi was so grief-stricken that she avoided eating for a couple of days. The interesting part of the case is that the relatives and her parents who killed the baby threw the entire blame on Meenakshi.

Meenakshi suffered from pangs of conscience. She felt she had committed a blunder, and she started praying to God to bless her with a male child. She was made to believe that she had sacrificed her girl child for getting a male child.

Meenakshi became pregnant again, after an interval of one year and was gifted with a male child. The couple and the parents were so happy that they celebrated the arrival of the new baby. Meenakshi underwent sterilization putting an end to the problem.

The case shows that motivation behind the killing was mainly poverty. The fear to face the future is one of the main causes of infanticide. The motivators in this case are not the couple but their immediate relatives.

Case Study—II

There is another case of female infanticide which also explained the killing with a religions overtone. Kasammal, the mother was married to Sokku Thevar and was residing in Sellur, Madurai, Kasammal and Sokku

Thevar were from Ariyapatti village of Usilampatti taluk. At the time of investigation Kasammal was about 35 years and her husband 40 years.

Though they were coming from an agricultural background they migrated to the city for want of occupation and they were doing business. Lending money was their side business. They also had some milch animals and they used to supply milk to the hotels. On an average they were earning thousand rupees a month. They can be classified as the upper middle income group.

Kasammal gave birth to seven children, all girls. However, the couple aspired for a male child. Each time they were gifted with a female child. During the interview with Kasammal and Sokku Thevar they revealed that four children had died between the ages of 3 and 5. No female child was killed by them till the sixth pregnancy. Kasammal became pregnant again for the seventh time. The couple, especially Kasammal, prayed for a male child. But she gave birth to a female child the seventh time also. During the eighth pregnancy Kasammal's mother-in-law arrived. She quoted the religious epics and she said to her son and daughter-in-law that the eight female child would ruin the family.

Thus the mother-in-law compelled Kasammal to kill the child if it is to be a female child. She narrated many religious stories to support that. Kasammal was mentally prepared to kill the baby child if it was a girl. Kasammal's mother-in-law cautioned her son also. Meanwhile Kasammal went atleast to a dozen temples and offered pooja to get a male child. Unfortunately the baby happened to be a female child against the wishes of the couple and the mother-in-law. Kasammal was very much attached to the child. Inspite of her protests, the child was killed.

Kasammal was helpless and she tried her best to protect her child. But her husband, mother-in-law and sisters-in-law started assaulting her physically. A grain of paddy was put into the baby's mouth and it was choked to death.

As far as this case is concerned, the motivating factor is not poverty but the decision imposed by the mother-in-law. The mother-in-law decided to kill the female baby thinking that it would bring ill-luck to the family. The mother tried till the last moment to protect the girl child though she failed in her attempt.

Case Study—III

Subbammal is the fifth daughter of Poochi Thevar and Perumayammal. She has four sisters and one elder brother. Bringing up the children proved to be burdensome for the parents of Subbammal. Poochi Thevar and Perumayammal were very poor, earning wages once in a while. Most of the days they starved for the sake of their children. Often they were not able to feed the children properly.

Poochi Thevar got all his daughters married with great difficulty. The society considered Poochi Thevar a good father. He performed all marriages simply in the village temple inviting only a few people. He got loans for each marriage but before the next marriage he repaid the loans. However after the fifth daughter's marriage Poochi Thevar became a pauper.

Subbammal was the last daughter of her parents and she was the pet of the father. She was loved not only by the parents but by all her sisters. She was looked after well because they believed that the fifth daughter would bring prosperity to the family.

Meanwhile Subbammal grew up into a beautiful girl and she married Karuppu Thevar who was working as a load man in a lorry. Karuppu Thevar was the maternal uncle of Subbammal. After marriage Subbammal was taken to Karuppu Thevar's house. Their life was happy in the beginning. As time passed she conceived. They were expecting a male child. Unfortunately subbammal delivered a female baby. Though Subbammal was happy to have a female child her husband and the relatives started ill-treating her for delivering a female child. Karuppu Thevar, an illiterate, coming from a very poor background, believed that it was Subbamal who was responsible for the female child. Whenever he saw the female child he started scolding Subbammal.

Meanwhile Subbammal conceived again and this time she was afraid of pregnancy and feared that she would again deliver a female baby. Subbammal became psychologically ill during pregnancy but she successfully completed her pregnancy and gave birth to a female child again. This was a shock to her as well as to her husband and to her relatives. They teased and scolded her for giving birth to another female child. Subbammal who had no role in deciding the sex of the issue felt unhappy but she brought her two daughters up with her own income. She did some manual jobs in order to raise money but still the question of killing child never came into the mind of Subbammal and her relatives. The condition of Subbammal and her daughters were so bad that she thought of ending her life several times. She would have ended her life but for her daughters.

The plight of Subbammal in Usilampatty during the time of pregnancy was such that the medical facilities were poor and contraception facilities were lacking. Subbammal became a victim of her husband's lust as a result of which she became pregnant again and again giving birth to six female children.

Subbammal herself was the fifth child of her parents and after Subbammal the parents got a male child. Subbammal believed that history would repeat itself. But in her case the sixth child was also a daughter. Subbammal became resigned. She left the decision to the relatives about the future of the sixth child. The relatives of Subbammal decided to kill the child instead of keeping it. Though Subbammal silently agreed to kill the child, she cried aloud when she saw her child taken away by her relatives.

Subbammal never slept during her seventh pregnancy as she was thinking of a similar predicament. Fortunately the seventh child was a male child. Her elder daughters were happy at having a small brother at last. Subbammal and her daughters admitted that they had never been to school because they were leading a hand-to-mouth existence.

Subbammal remembers even now the murder she had agreed to. The motivating factor in this case is the pressure of the relatives. If the mother of the child had been a little courageous she could have saved the child. However the mental condition of the mother was so bad she left her child to the mercy of the relatives immediately after delivery.

As far as her husband is concerned his only motive is to get a male child. He never wanted to kill the girl child though he was also a silent witness to the killing of his own daughter by the relatives. His attitude towards female infanticide is mere indifference.

Case Study—IV

Chakkaraipatti is near Usilampatti village where Thavasi Thevar set up his family. Thavasi Thevar married Kamayee and they had two daughters. The parents got the two daughters married.

Veerammal is the name of the second daughter of Thavasi Thevar. Veerammal was married to Pandi at the age of 15 and they moved from Sakkaraipatti to Thathaneri. Pandi ran a small mutton stall there. So they had good income to make both ends meet. Pandi was a follower of Gandhi and his principles. They never went for luxury, but lived a simple life. Veerammal and Pandi had two daughters and a son.

After a long interval Veerammal became pregnant again. The pregnancy itself was unwanted as they already had two daughters and a son. However they did not go for abortion and decided to have the fourth child. The son criticized his mother for pregnant at the stage of life. At the time of the fourth pregnancy Veerammal was about 35 years and her son was about 10. So after the interval of 10 years Veerammal became pregnant. Society looked down upon her. She was prepared to bring the child up irrespective of its sex. The neighbour pitied Veerammal so much that they started educating her about the consequence of giving birth to a female child.

Neighbours told her that she already had two daughters and if she had another female baby she would suffer a lot. She started believing that the fourth girl would trouble the mother during the seventh and the eight month of pregnancy. She had some trouble during three months and Veerammal became convinced that the baby girl would bring real trouble to her. Therefore, she became mentally prepared to kill the child if it were a girl.

Veerammal gave birth and as she feared, the child was a girl. She didn't kill the child immediately. She became restless, and she poured hot chicken soup into the mouth of the baby which killed the baby instantly.

The neighbours and the relatives came to know of the incident the next day. The mother herself committed the offence and she became psychologically ill from that day onwards.

As far as this case is concerned the mother is the one who was responsible for killing the female child. No body urged the mother to kill the girl child. Psychological fear forced the mother to kill her child.

In this case the exact role played by the husband was not revealed either by the wife or the relatives.

Conclusion

In all the four cases the reasons are different ranging from economic to social concerns though the major reason seems to be economic. Poverty is the curse of this group. Majority of the people belong to the lower economic group. Secondly it is the pressure given by the outsiders which motivates the mother to kill the child or cause it to be killed.

As Dahrendorf said "a false consciousness is created by the individual in order to legitimize certain issues."[5] Though Dahrendorf uses the theory in the Industrial Section to refer to the workers' practices, it is applicable to all mothers involved directly or indirectly in infanticide.

Notes :

1. S. Gurusamy, S. C. Kubendran, "A Decade for the Girl Child (1991-2000)", *Social Welfare*, Vol. XXXVII , No. 11-12, February - March 1991, p. 16.
2. *Indian Express Magazine*, October 28, 1990, p. 1.
3. The terms Pothum Ponnu, Pothumadi and Pothumani used in Tamil can be translated to mean "enough of girl child".
4. S. Gurusamy and S. C. Kubendran, *op. cit.*, p. 16.
5. Ruth A. Wallace, *Contemporary Sociological Theory*, 1980, pp. 121-132.

3

Infanticide and the Immediate Society

Introduction

The Indian Society is one of the most complex because of its structure. Majority of the Indian population live in underdeveloped areas which are referred to as rural areas. The underdevelopment is in terms of style of living, attitude to living, and the use of resources in living. According to 1990-91 Census, of 627,146,597 people 74.28 percent lived in villages.

Indian Rural Scene

The Indian rural area is dominated by concepts of family, caste systems and rituals. Even the secondary social institutions namely polity and religion depend upon the primary social institutions like caste, family and the village community. Primary social institutions as well as the secondary social institutions are very much oriented towards the value systems prevailing in the village community which in turn are adopted by the rural people. The caste system is the base of rural life and the caste composition has the greatest significance in the social context. In the traditional society caste system and class system are synonyms, the upper caste being the upper class and the lower class being the lower caste. The inter-caste relations are very much affected by the caste compositions prevailing in the village. The economic and political changes are very much associated with the caste structure of the village. The land relations are also based on caste. The upper caste people control the production of the village and the lower caste people are totally dependent on them. The result is that the lower castes have a permanent poverty-culture in a rural society. The rural indebtedness is a problem because the money lender and middle men exploit the rural agricultural scene which in course of time makes most of the lower income group in the rural area indebted permanently to the upper caste.

Just as economics is very much related to the caste system, the politics also is related to it. The village administration and the village leadership are controlled by upper caste people. Caste councils and village councils are the political features of traditional rural India whereas community development programmes and Panchayati Raj are the features of modern political systems in the rural India. Both traditional and the modern political organisations in villages are dominated by caste rules as the upper castes are economically are and religiously superior.

The religious supremacy of the various caste has given rise to a value system in the rural society. The model of rural India is also geared to the expectations of the villages. The belief system of Indian religion and the consequent customs, norms, mores or folk-ways are the guiding factors of rural India. Thus one can see both the positive and the negative sides of Indian culture in the villages of India. The Family and kinship are given much importance by the villagers and as a result the family and kinship-oriented functions are emphasized. The Life-cycle ceremonies are the festivals of kindred. Most of the life-cycle ceremonies of the villages are celebrated by all the relatives together.

Apart from celebrating the life-cycle ceremonies, customs like child marriage, caste endogamy, village exogamy and preferential marriages are prevailing in Indian villages. Most of the customs and traditions affect the weaker sections of the community, namely the lower caste people and women.

The problems of rural society are economic and social in nature. Most of the social problems are in one way or the other related to women. The problems like preferential marriage, caste exogamy, village exogamy, and community marriage are all patriarchal in nature. If one analysis deeply the village structure namely caste, family etc., one can find that they are male oriented.

In most of the Indian villages the basic units are caste, family and kinship. The villages of Tamil Nadu have certain peculiar customs like preferential marriages. Tamil Nadu villages are a clustership in nature and they form both miraci and "Innam" villages. The caste structure is made up of the Brahmin and the non-Brahmins. The Brahmins are the upper caste and the non Brahmins are the lower or service caste or Harijans.

Rural Areas in Tamil Nadu

Roughly, in Tamil Nadu, rural area form 65.80 per cent. Table 3.1 shows the rural and urban distribution of population.

Table 3.1 : Distribution of Population in Rural and Urban Areas

Year	*Rural*		*Urban*		*Total Population*	
	Male	*Female*	*Male*	*Female*	*Male*	*Female*
1971	14438727 (35.1%)	14295607 (34.1%)	6389294 (15.5%)	6075540 (14.7%)	20828041 (50.6%)	20371147 (49.4%)
1981	16280081 (33.6%)	16089423 (33.4%)	8140147 (17%)	7787805 (16%)	24420228 (50.6%)	23877228 (49.4%)
1991	18466088 (33.7%)	18145197 (32.5%)	9751859 (17.3%)	9275147 (16.5%)	28217947 (51%)	27420371 (49%)

Source : 1971 and 1981 Census Publication.
1991 Census Publication (Provisional Population Totals)

The rural areas, mainly agricultural, depend on rain water for cultivation. The agricultural economics and resultant social system reveal the characteristics of the rural people.

Caste, kinship and family form the basic factors of rural life. Caste structure is the social structure of the villagers and therefore caste determines the position of the people in the village. Caste also influences the economy because it is the upper-caste people in the villages who possess a major share of the land. The pattern of agriculture is such that majority of the villagers dependent upon a few people who own the land.

The rural areas of Tamil Nadu are mainly divided into three, Garden land, dry land and wet land. When the wet land has three crops in a year, garden land usually has one wet crop and one dry crop, and dry land has only the dry crop. In the field men as well as women work in different capacities. However the women-folk normally get less wages than men. The Minimum Wages Act has been introduced in Tamil Nadu. Still women continue to get only less wages than men. Besides, women get work only if there is more work than what men can manage. When the work is scarce, they are not employed.

This economic structure affects the schedule castes, and the schedule tribes also. The illiteracy among women is more.

The rural girls are seldom sent for higher education. Once the girls attains puberty either they are given away in marriage or they are made to do odd jobs at home.

Most of the life cycle ceremonies affect women as they are the target or the cause of the ceremony. The life cycle ceremony changes the status of the family according to the way they celebrate it. Therefore each ritual or ceremony is given importance by the family and the village. The birth ceremony, marriage ceremony and death ceremony are considered important occasions to show off the status of the family in the society. The economic affordability of the parents become immaterial, when celebrating domestic functions. The village does not place high the status of an individual if marriages are not celebrated properly. Each ceremony costs a huge amount of money which affects the economic status of the family. The family usually spends all its savings on domestic ceremonies but not an education or employment of the children.

Thus the villagers of Tamil Nadu consider the community ceremonies more important than their own development. The rural society of Tamil Nadu has not progressed due to this factor. The rural society has not changed much though social changes are occurring at a fast rate. The social change in rural society is one-sided. The green revolution and other modernizations have given a lift to the economic but this benefit is by and large enjoyed only by the upper class sections of the rural society. The legal measures like Land Reforms Act, the Minimum Wages Act, the agricultural co-operatives and rural banking system have helped only very little as far as the rural lower people are concerned. Thus, the rural upper class people who are benefited by social changes are economically better and so they are the custodians of the social structure. These people follow all the customs and beliefs which usually become the guiding principles of the rural society. The lower class and lower caste of the rural society follow these people as their models and observe their social values as far as possible. In this process the losers are the low caste people who are becoming poorer day by day. In this context one can say that it is the lack of proper orientation which is responsible for the lack of change in the attitudes of the rural people.

Attitudes of Women Towards Changing Their Status

The terms status, equality, justice, position etc., are loosely used to denote the ranking of women in society. All these terms have meanings according to the contexts in which they are used. The terms are used to compare women's position with that of men. Therefore these terms have to be analysed in depth in understand the political, social, philosophical, economic and religious significance denoted by these terms.

Status is used more commonly in the static aspect of a role, each status having its own role. The status is inclusive of many factors as it is multi-dimensional.

The status refers to both sociological as well as psychological aspects. Neither social aspects nor psychological aspects alone can give the right status for the individual.

Society is the most responsible factor for changing the position of an individual. The position in the society is based on certain factors which the society feels as important. As far as woman's position is concerned the basic belief system of the society, namely religion is the pivotal aspect determining the position. This is exactly true as far as rural society is concerned. In rural India modernisation is one-sided. The economic changes have not affected the social factors. So the society remains unchanged in rural India making woman's position inferior. The concept of equality has not spread to the rural society. Equality, which is again a relative term, is very much associated with social values. A rural woman cannot believe in the concept of equality because the concept itself is alien to rural culture. The development measures, namely, voluntary welfare schemes and government projects have provided little to emphasis the concept of equality. Equality and status are considered different and it is difficult to bring about an understanding among the rural people that equality would lead to status. Status is considered a position in the society and therefore if a individual is elevated by certain measures it is considered a higher status. In the case of women, status is not elevation but bringing about equality of the sexes in the social, economic, political and religious contexts. The main goal is to achieve social justice for women on par with that of men.

Rural women's attitude are greatly influenced by religion. Religious values are internalized by women during the socialization process which in turn gives them the values of life. The informal education of the rural society begins during the early childhood, which is the main means of passing the age-old religious values to the next generation. This attitude is thus a permanent phenomenon in the rural society. There is no diversification in the attitude because of the closed system. Changes in the rural society are concerned only with the economic aspect bordering on the social factors. Education, economic development and political modernisation have brought changes in the structural aspect of Tamil Nadu. The weaker sections of the society are unaltered by these changes.

Women of rural Tamil Nadu can be classified into three types. The first category are those who are educated in urban centres. The second category are the group of women who are educated in rural schools or colleges. The third category of women are illiterate women. With regard to the first category of women the urban influences have changed their physical and mental outlook. The elite women in the rural areas looks down upon other women and at the same time they will not take any initiative to improve the lot of other women but take the earliest opportunity to move to urban centres. These women adopt the values of urban areas. This category shows a psychological alienation which creates a gap between their rural make-up and urban values.

Women who are educated in rural schools rarely try to change the attitudes existing in the villages. For them, education is a means of reducing the dowry or of getting employment. The women of this category consider education only a secondary social phenomenon, the primary being the values of society.

In order to understand the various groups of women one has to analyse the socio-economic background. The female infanticide is to be understood against the back-drop of social and economic issues.

Socio-economic Background of Women in the Selected Two Villages

Nadumuthalaikulam and Kuppanapatti are the two villages selected for the study from which sixty women were taken for intensive analysis. The attitude changes of the sixty women is used as the experimental method. Therefore it is necessary to know the socio-economic background of these women. The total number of households in these villages is 596, of which 362 are in Nadumuthalaikulam and 234 in Kuppanampatti.

Table 3.2 : Population of the Two Villages

Villages	*Male*	*Female*	*Total*
Kuppanampatti (Control Village)	727 (51.63%)	681 (48.3%)	1408 100%)
Nadumuthalaikulam (Experimental Village)	766 (57.29%)	571 (42.71%)	1337 (100%)

Source : Field Work.

The male female ratio in the two villages is 51.63%, 48.37% and 57.29%, 42.71% respectively the former representing Kuppanampatti and the latter Nadumuthalaikulam. The male-female ratio shows that it is adverse to women. There are only 42.71% females for 57.29% males in Nadumuthalaikulam and 48.37% for 51.63% in Kuppanampatti village. The ratio of women to men deteriorated over the past twenty years due to several reasons.

Table 3.3 shows that the number of women are less in these villages.

Table 3.3 : Male Female Ratio from 1971 onwards

(Values in Percentage)

Year	*Control Village*			*Experimental Village*		
	Male	*Female*	*Total*	*Male*	*Female*	*Total*
1971	40.27	59.73	100	45.36	54.64	100
1981	44.74	55.25	100	48.52	51.48	100
1991	51.63	48.37	100	57.63	42.71	100

The women selected for the study belongs to the age group of 15-35, and this group is an experimental group for measuring the attitude-change.

This group is selected purposely because it is this group who are going to the future mothers. There is an urgent need to change the attitude of these women.

By and large the villages are most backward and the people are illiterate. Added to this there is a social restriction for women in these villages. There is a strong belief in the village against girls going for education which explains the dwindling number of girls studying in educational institutions.

It is also found that education is not considered a tool for to change in these villages. The sample shows that 57.5% of women are illiterate whereas only 42.5% are semi-literate. Those who are educated have studied only upto the primary level. There is not even a single case in the sample who is educated above the primary level.

Table 3.4 : Literacy Level of the Villages

Sl. No.	*Category*	*Control Village*	*Experimental Village*	*Total*
1.	Illiterate	33 (55%)	36 (60%)	69 (57.5%)
2.	Semi-literate	27 (45%)	24 (40%)	51 (42.5%)
	Total	*60 (100%)*	*60 (100%)*	*120 (110%)*

There is a correlation between age and education. The younger age group has a positive approach towards education whereas the older group does not consider education a means for progress. The variables like marriage, family income and occupation play a crucial role in the attitude formations. The girls even before marriage understand the problems of being a girl. Though they are brought up along with other children they are conscious of their sex.

It is interesting to note the marital background of women of these villages. Most of the villagers have not recorded the age of the girls. They calculate their age approximately according to the time of their reaching puberty, that is between the years 13 and 18. These girls usually forms their attitude only during this stage. During the early part of marriage itself, the girls face many problems from their husbands and families. Some girls even before the age of 20 get socially and psychologically frustrated that they hate not only themselves but the whole society. In this process the first person she hates is her own daughter. She sees her image in daughter and she wants to make her escape life's problems. Female infanticide is a handy solution for this. It is this attitude that has to change into a positive approach. The only solution for this is to change the attitude of the young mother towards her future, towards motherhood and towards life itself. It is important to change the attitude of unmarried girls by educating them. Education can be given through the socialisation process in a traditional way which the elders think to be the correct way. Each generation is a replica of the previous generation. Unless the social background is changed through education one can not visualize any change.

The economic background of the villagers is equally bad as their social condition. The monthly income of an average household in the village is around Rupees 250 per month. Majority of the people in these two villages are agricultural coolies. These people get the full employment only during agricultural seasons. The rest of the time they are unemployed or underemployed. Usually men, women and children go to work during seasons but at other times women and children remain unemployed. The income of the selected group falls into two categories, the group which earns between 200 and 300 and the group which earns a little more.

Table 3.5 : Occupational Structure of the Villages

Sl. No.	Category	Control Village	Experimental Village	Total
1.	Agriculture (ownership)	27 (45%)	25 (41.7%)	52 (43.33%)
2.	Agricultural Cooley	27 (45%)	28 (46.7%)	5 (45.83%)
3.	Others	6 (10%)	7 (11.7%)	13 (10.83%)
	Total	**60 (100%)**	**60 (100%)**	**120 (110%)**

Table 3.6 : Income Structure of the Villages

Sl. No.	*Category (Rs.)*	*Control Village*	*Experimental Village*	*Total*
1.	Below 200	20 (33.3%)	49 (81.7%)	69 (57.5%)
2.	201 to 450	39 (65%)	11 (18.3%)	50 (41.66%)
3.	Above 401	1 (1%)	---	1 (0.83%)
	Total	**60 (100%)**	**60 (100%)**	**120 (99.99%)**

Caste councils exist in society irrespective of social changes that have taken place in a village. Women of these villages consider caste councils as the most important political institution. Caste councils are given much importance by the villagers. It is the caste council which advises them. Today the villages have the benefit of different programmes such as mother-care, child care, and free medical facilities. Co-operative Societies help the village in improving agriculture by giving loans, seeds, manure, pesticides etc.

In Nadumuthalaikulam and Kuppanampatti women say that they have not utilized Government programmes fully. They do not know the reason but one can infer that it is the prevailing attitude of the society which prevents them from availing the benefits of such programmes, as they are illiterate. They do not understand fully the merits of such programmes. This is one of the greatest disadvantages women are facing. There is nobody to make them aware and nobody to train them and prepare them to face the changing needs of the society. Here only education can act as a saviour.

Education should be given a greater role in changing women in the villages of India. Formal as well as the informal education should be imparted to the villagers. In Nadumuthalaikulam and Kuppanampatti education is denied to women. Girls are not sent to school. Women are not offered adult education or social education. They are yet to understand the role of education in modernising the self. At the same time it is to be noted that the villagers know that education is a must to improve the life-style. Thus in both villages the respondents say that education is necessary for improving themselves.

Table 3.7 : Education is Necessary for the Family Members

Sl. No.	*Category*	*Control Village*	*Experimental Village*	*Total*
1.	Necessary	48 (80%)	41 (68.3%)	89 (74.2%)
2.	Not necessary	12 (20%)	19 (31.7%)	31 (25.83%)
	Total	*60 (100%)*	*60 (100%)*	*120 (100%)*

They say that now it is very difficult for them without education even to sign their names. They also believe that education is necessary for writing letters, reading letters, cinema poster, and the bus numbers. From this one can understand that they are keen to learn the three R's.

The villages women also know about the educational programmes for the adults. They told the investigator that they were aware of the adults' education programme. The only drawback here is that there is no motivation for them to attend the adult education programme. Most of the time they are busy with domestic work. Women in these villages cannot spare time for such programmes as they are engaged in the kitchen and in the field all the time. Many of them expressed their desire to learn through adult education.

Women think that they can progress by engaging in some economic activities. They want to train themselves in motor mechanism, cottage industries, bakery, tailoring etc., They say that such training will help them attain independence.

Most of the respondents were positive towards adult education and it is in this context that adult education was introduced in Nadumuthalikulam.

As the income of the family is very little, the family is split into nuclear families. Today the village consists of mostly nuclear families. Only 20 per cent of women live a joint family. Though the families are nuclear, the families are united because most of the families live in the same village or in the neighbouring villages. Here again a woman is bound to tradition and she has to satisfy all the kin groups though she is in a nuclear family.

The socio-economic background of the woman reveals that the villages they come from are backward and offer very little opportunity for the advancement of women. The villagers find that even two square meals a day are a luxury. All these conditions affect the progress of women in the villages and the conditions in which they live.

Women and Society

From the discussion above, it is clear that women and the larger society two different. The society of women differ from the larger society, because the value systems existing in these two are different. The system forces the women to be different from the larger social system. The collective consciousness of the society and the collective consciousness of illiterate women instead of superimposing on each other are separated from each other. Though the women in the selected villages accept that there are leisure-time activities it is with restrictions only they are allowed to take part in it. Folklore in various forms provides recreation for women. When men engage themselves in gambling, going to films etc., women usually spend their leisure time in witnessing street plays, participating in Kummy etc., which are performed occasionally in a year in the village. Women say that there are various forms of folklore in the village and they are interested in such activities.

It is disheartening to note that women in Nadumuthalaikulam and Kuppanampatti are not involved in the decision-making process. They do not know the problems or the solutions. The basic needs of women are water and health. The two problems specified by women are common to both the villages. The major problems according to them are lack of drinking water, transport facilities, schools and health centres. These are the problems with which women are concerned.

4

Attitude of Women Towards Female Infanticide

In the control village Kuppanampatti, where sixty house holds were selected for study it was found that women were not given the benefits of adult education. The village, Kuppanampatti, is far away from the experimental village Nadumuthalaikulam, and therefore the adult education process functioning in the experimental village had no impact on the control village. The purpose of choosing a control village is to study the effects of the experiment under well defined conditions. After five months the study was repeated in both the experimental and the control villages. The results of the study before and after the experiments are given in the fifth and the sixth chapters.

In both the villages the sixty households were divided into two units of 30 each, to facilitate easy analysis. After stratifying the households, various adult education kits were administered to the households in the control village. The control village was kept away from any external influences.

Kuppanampatti, the control village is 20 km away from the town which has two schools, one agriculture bank and one co-operative society. Most of the villagers are illiterate having different types of attitude towards themselves and towards women. The researcher concentrated on women as this village is a high-rate area of female infanticide. The main aim of this study is to know the impact of adult education on women. The change is measured at two intervals, that is before the experiment of adult education and after. Attitude which is more a psychological phenomenon is influenced and changed periodically by external factors. But certain basic attitudes remain the same.

Generally a basic attitude is referred to as a permanent attitude. Formation of the attitude is mostly a consequence of the socialisation process which is internalised early in the individual. These internalization processes are so strong that they lead to a permanent attitude formation in the individual. Thus attitude towards the girl child, attitude towards literacy, attitude towards self-reliance and attitude towards female infanticide remain permanent in the minds of the people. In Kuppanampatti, women are treated as second-class citizens because attitude towards women in the area is mostly negative in nature. Women are not respected by the society and the family. In such underdeveloped areas women loss their self-confidence and esteem.

Society in Kuppanampatti is mostly patriarchal in nature, and hence the attitude also is patriarchal in nature. Though the women in the village are interested in progress and change, no opportunity is given to them because of male-resistance. Four different types of attitudes were identified in the village out of which two relate to literacy, and the girl child. The attitudes towards self-reliance and female infanticide form the other two. These attitudes were studied among the women of Kuppanampatti, 30 years and below. This was purposely done because after 30 years it is difficult to change the attitude. As far as literacy is concerned in the control village there was no change after six months. In the first thirty houses there was no change, but in the second cluster which consists of 30 houses there was a low attitude towards literacy. In the village (control - Kuppanampatti) the mean during the first study was 7.10 and after the study the mean was 6.90 (Appendix I) whereas in the second study the sample mean was 7.37 and 6.03 (Appendix II) respectively. From the mean value it can be inferred that the women of Kuppanampatti had a negative attitude towards literacy and this continued to exist even after six months. Here one should remember that there was not much change either internally or externally in this village, so the attitude remained the same. Still in the village the attitude towards literacy came down from 7.37 to 6.03 which is one of the significant points. Even among the younger generation, the value of education or the value of literacy has not reached them in the right manner.

In societies like Kuppanampatti where education can play a big role, the awareness is not high.

In Kuppanampatti the same trend is seen after six months also. In fact many people joined the "not necessary" group after the experiment. 96.7 per cent of the women felt that education was not necessary for them. Only two women remained neutral who belonged to the younger age group. As education was not given to the women from a very long time the importance of education was not known to them or to the society.

Table 4.1 : Attitude of the Women Towards the Statement "Education is Necessary for Woman"

After Experiment—Control Village

Respondents	*Neutral*	*Not Essential*	*Total*
Below 20	2 7.1	26 92.9	28 46.7
21 to 30		27 100.0 46.6	27 45.0
Above		5 100.0 8.6	5 8.3
Total	*2* *3.3*	*58* *96.7*	*60* *100*

Chi-square = 2.36453 Min. E.F. = .167
D.F. = 2 Cells with E.F.<5 = 4 of 6 (66.7%)
Significance = .3066 Number of Missing observations = 0

Education in the rural society differs from mere literacy. Most of the women do not know how to live on in their immediate surroundings. Women of Kuppanampatti lead a poverty-stricken life, with a meagre earning of ten rupees or less a day. Education and literacy are significantly low. 63.3 per cent of the women before the experiment denied the relationship between literacy and education. According to them literacy would not help education. However, a married and illiterate women belonging to the lower income group said that there was a relationship between literacy and education.

This women who had believed in a positive relationship between education and literacy was aware of the adult education programme. Many women do not know the difference between literacy and education. Such women remained neutral when asked about the relationship between these two concepts 35 per cent in the pre-study and 48.3 per cent in the post-study periods remained neutral as they were not able to answer the question regarding the relationship.

The women of Kuppanampatti without knowing the importance of education have led a peaceful life but from the angle of the larger society, education being one of the most important components of progress, it was felt that education should be given to everybody. Even the ignorant and the illiterate should be made aware of the importance of education. Table 5.3 shows that 56.7 per cent of the women of this village did not accept that education was necessary for progress. They see education and progress as two separate entities. Education is considered by them as a tool for developing the personality whereas progress is considered as economic progress. They are not able to associate themselves with the view that education can improve their style of living. Majority of the women (except 6.7% in the pre study and 5% in the post study) did not agree that there was a relationship between economic progress and Education. All the women above 30 either remained silent or disagreed with the issue of progress.

As education was not given importance in the society under study school education was not considered an important vehicle for progress. Even today the women of Kuppanampatti do not send their children to school. The only attraction in the school is the meals given during the day not the knowledge imparted there. The school education is given least importance as one can see that 68.3 per cent of the women do not consider school education necessary to eradicate illiteracy.

Women of Kuppanampatti do not believe that they can attain literacy and education through Schooling. They like to become literate if they are given an opportunity. 28.3 per cent of women in the pre-study have categorically declared that they would become literate if they were given an opportunity. Women who belong to different socio-economic background are included here. After six months 41.7 per cent of the women expressed a neutral idea when asked the same question.

Education is one of the tools of modernisation and literacy is one of the components of education. Though this is realised by the women folk of rural India, it is the society which prohibits women from entering the school system. Most of the rural women are not aware of the importance of literacy for their development. In Indian society girls are not sent to school or they are withdrawn after 3 or 4 years. Both Central and State Governments are taking all the steps to improve the education of women but the social factors remain the same. Besides it is difficult to increase the strength in schools. There is a clear-cut differentiation in the enrolment number of boys and girls in the Indian rural educational system. Boys are given importance during childhood which is continued throughout life.

The present study found that 48.3 per cent of the women in the pre-study and 50 per cent of women in the post-study were of the opinion that education is necessary only for boys. A significant number of women still have the traditional attitude towards the concept of equality of the sexes (Table 4.2 and 4.2A).

The same opinion was reversed when asked about the necessity of giving education for girls. 38.3 per cent of the women in the pre-study and 46.7 per cent in post-study did not believe in girl's education. One of the significant findings is that in the post study only 8.3 per cent of the women said that education was necessary for girls. This number is comparatively low from that of the pre-study.

In the post-study it was found that there was an association between the socio-economic background and attitude towards girls education. Those who had higher income and status did not send their girls to school for education. They preferred getting them married early in life. This group of people, in the post-study, revealed that they did sent their girls to education because of the fear of social disapproval. 41.7 per cent of the women and 68.3 per cent of the women in the pre-study and post-study respectively questioned the necessity of education when there was a sound economic background. Education and economy are not considered complementary to each other. It is the upper income group which does not believe in education for girls. Similarly, education and marriage were differentiated by the rural women. Most of them believed that education and marriage were two different things and they preferred marriage to education. 40 per cent of the women in the pre-study and 45 per cent of the women in post-study express this opinion but there was a some change in the opinion in the post-study. 51.7 per cent of the women in the post-study agreed that education was necessary for girls for leading a happy married life (Table 4.4 and 4.A).

Table 4.2 : Attitude of the Women Towards the Statement "Education is Necessary only for Boys"

Before Experiment—Control Village

Respondents	*Agree*	*Neutral*	*Disagree*	*Total*
	14	4	9	27
Below 20	51.9	14.8	33.3	45.0
	48.3	30.8	50.0	
	12	8	8	28
21 to 30	42.9	28.6	28.6	46.7
	41.4	61.5	44.4	
	3	1	1	5
Above 31	60.0	20.0	20.0	8.3
	10.3	7.7	5.6	
	29	*13*	*18*	*60*
Total	*48.3*	*21.7*	*30.0*	*100*

Chi-square = 1.87697 D.F. = 4
Significance = .7584 Min. E.F. = 1.083
Cells with E.F.<5 = 3 of 9 (33.3%) No. of Missing observations = 0

Table 4.2A : Attitude of the Women Towards the Statement "Education is Necessary only for Boys"

After Experiment—Control Village

Respondents	*Agree*	*Neutral*	*Disagree*	*Total*
	14	4	10	28
Below 20	50.0	14.3	35.7	46.7
	46.7	66.7	41.7	
	12	2	13	27
21 to 30	44.4	7.4	48.1	45.0
	40.0	33.3	54.2	
	4		1	5
Above 31	80.0		20.0	8.3
	13.3		4.2	
	30	*6*	*24*	*60*
Total	*50.0*	*10.0*	*40.0*	*100*

Chi-square = 3.33915 D.F. = 4
Significance = .5028 Min. E.F. = .500
Cells with E.F.<5 = 5 of 9 (55.6%) No. of Missing observations = 0

Table 4.3 : Attitude of the Women Towards the Statement "Education is Necessary for Girls Too"

Before Experiment—Control Village

Respondents	*Agree*	*Neutral*	*Disagree*	*Total*
	6	9	12	27
Below 20	22.2	33.3	44.4	45.0
	35.3	45.0	52.2	
	9	9	10	28
21 to 30	32.1	32.1	35.7	46.7
	52.9	45.0	43.5	
	2	2	1	5
Above 31	40.0	40.0	20.0	8.3
	11.8	10.0	4.3	
	17	*20*	*23*	*60*
Total	*28.3*	*33.3*	*38.3*	*100*

Chi-square = 1.56962 Min. E.F. = 1.417
D.F. = 4 Cells with E.F.<5 = 3 of 9 (33.3%)
Significance = .8142 No. of Missing observations = 0

Table 4.3A : Attitude of the Women Towards the Statement "Education is Necessary for Girls Too"

After Experiment—Control Village

Respondents	**Agree**	**Neutral**	**Disagree**	**Total**
	4	14	10	28
Below 20	14.3	50.0	35.7	46.7
	80.0	51.9	35.7	
	1	10	16	27
21 to 30	3.7	37.0	59.3	45.0
	20.0	37.0	57.1	
		3	2	5
Above 31		60.0	40.0	8.3
		11.1	7.1	
	5	*27*	*28*	*60*
Total	*8.3*	*45.0*	*46.7*	*100*

Chi-square = 4.77240 Min. E.F. = .417
D.F. = 4 Cells with E.F.<5 = 53 of 9 (55.6%)
Significance = .3115 No. of Missing observations = 0

Table 4.4 : Attitude of the Women Towards the Statement "Education is Necessary for girls for Leading a Happy Married Life"

Before Experiment—Control Village

Respondents	Agree	Neutral	Disagree	Total
Below 20	11 40.7 47.8	6 22.2 46.2	10 37.0 41.7	27 45.0
21 to 30	8 28.6 34.8	7 25.0 53.8	13 46.4 54.2	28 46.7
Above 31	4 80.0 17.4		1 20.0 4.2	5 8.3
Total	*23* *38.3*	*13* *21.7*	*24* *40.0*	*60* *100*

Chi-square = 5.08070 Min. E.F. = 1.083
D.F. = 4 Cells with E.F.<5 = 3 of 9 (33.3%)
Significance = ..2791 No. of Missing observations = 0

Table 4.4A : Attitude of the Women Towards the Statement "Education is Necessary for girls for Leading a Happy Married Life"

After Experiment—Control Village

Respondents	*Agree*	*Neutral*	*Disagree*	*Total*
Below 20	15 53.6 48.4	2 7.1 100.0	11 39.3 40.7	28 46.7
21 to 30	14 51.9 45.2		13 48.1 48.1	27 45.0
Above 31	2 40.0 6.5		3 60.0 11.1	5 8.3
Total	*31* *51.7*	*2* *3.3*	*27* *45.0*	*60* *100*

Chi-square = 2.94992 Min. E.F. = .167
D.F. = 4 Cells with E.F.<5 = 5 of 9 (55.6%)
Significance = ..5662 No. of Missing observations = 0

The knowledge through education is not only for writing or reading but also it can be used for facing the calamities of life. Even the rural people believed that education would enlighten women. Self-confidence is gained through education. 40 per cent of the women in Kuppanampatti said that education was necessary to met the calamities of life.

Table 4.5 : Attitude of the Women Towards the Statement "Education is Necessary to Meet the Calamities of Life"

Before Experiment—Control Village

Respondents	*Agree*	*Neutral*	*Disagree*	*Total*
	11	4	12	27
Below 20	40.7	14.8	44.4	45.0
	45.8	28.6	54.5	
	11	10	7	28
21 to 30	39.3	35.7	25.0	46.7
	45.8	71.4	31.8	
	2		3	5
Above 31	40.0		60.0	8.3
	8.3		13.6	
Column	*24*	*14*	*22*	*60*
Total	*40.0*	*23.3*	*36.7*	*100*

Chi-square	= 6.08035	Min. E.F.	= 1.167
D.F.	= 4	Cells with E.F.<5 =	3 of 9 (33.3%)
Significance	= .1932	No. of Missing observations = 0	

As far as education was concerned the number of women who attached importance to education was meagre. India is expecting to achieve 100 per cent literacy within a few years but even half of the population do not have a positive attitude towards education.

The analysis shows that attitude towards literacy is not encouraging in the Kuppanampatti village. As this village is a control village the attitude remains the same in the pre-study as well as in the post-study period. There was not much change within the intervening period of six months. Women of Kuppanmapatti still have a traditional outlook on education.

The traditional out-look is seen not only in the field of education but also in their attitude to girl-child, life-style etc. As mentioned earlier the

Table 4.5A : Attitude of the Women Towards the Statement "Education is Necessary to Meet the Calamities of Life"

After Experiment—Control Village

Respondents	*Agree*	*Neutral*	*Disagree*	*Total*
	12	8	8	28
Below 20	42.9	28.6	28.6	46.7
	46.2	38.1	61.5	
	12	12	3	27
21 to 30	44.4	44.4	11.1	45.0
	46.2	57.1	23.1	
	2	1	2	5
Above 31	40.0	20.0	40.0	8.3
	7.7	4.8	15.4	
	26	*21*	*13*	*60*
Total	*43.3*	*35.0*	*21.7*	*100*

Chi-square	= 4.14233	Min. E.F.	= 1.083
D.F.	= 4	Cells with E.F.<5 =	3 of 9 (33.3%)
Significance	= .3871	No. of Missing observations = 0	

concept of equality or gender justice is still not dominant for the people of Kuppanampatti. Girls and women are considered only secondary citizens in the rural areas. This is because of the system of beliefs existing within the Hindu society. According to the Hindu scriptures only the sons can take their parents to heaven by lighting the funeral pyre. Therefore, Hindu families consider a son essential for the last rites. This opinion was expressed by all the respondents of Kuppanampatti. The same result was seen in the pre-study as well as in the post-study. The study was conducted among the Thevars of Usilampatti and this caste is unique in having certain customs. It is believed that the women of this caste have exemplary character and courage. Though usually it is not a Practice for the girls to light the funeral pyre, 91.7 percent of women in the pre-study and 98.3 per cent in the post study agreed that if there was no male child the female child could perform the funeral rites. It is to be noted here that this practice is peculiar to this community.

Among Thevars even in the traditional Society, women used to perform the funeral rites in the absence of men. This is due to the custom prevailing in the community that those who are lighting the funeral pyre is the legal heir to the properties of the dead person.

Male children are considered an asset to the family by the Thevar community. This is because of the fact that the males bring in money and offer protection. 93.3 per cent of the women had such an opinion.

Table 4.6 : Attitude of the Women Towards the Statement "Male Children Bring Money to the Family"

Before Experiment—Control Village

Respondents	*Agree*	*Neutral*	*Total*
Below 20	25 92.6 44.6	2 7.4 50.0	27 45.0
21 to 30	26 92.9 46.4	2 7.1 50.0	28 46.7
Above 31	5 100 8.9		5 8.3
Total	*56* *93.3*	*4* *6.7*	*60* *100*

Chi-square = .39116 Min. E.F. = .333
D.F. = 2 Cells with E.F.<5 = 4 of 6 (66.7%)
Significance = .8224 Number of observations = 0

Table 4.6A : Attitude of the Women Towards the Statement "Male Children Bring Money to the Family"

Before Experiment—Control Village

Respondents	*Agree*	*Neutral*	*Total*
Illiterate	31 93.9 55.4	2 6.1 50.0	33 55.0
Semi-literate	25 92.6 44.6	2 7.4 50.0	27 45.0
Total	*56* *93.3*	*4* *6.7*	*60* *100*

Chi-square = .00000 .04329 Min. E.F. = 1.800
D.F. = 1 1 Cells with E.F.<5 = 2 of 4 (50.0%)
Significance= 1.0000 .8352 (Before Yates
Number of Missing observations = 0 Correction)

Table 4.6B : Attitude of the Women Towards the Statement "Male Children Bring Money to the Family"

Before Experiment—Control Village

Respondents	*Agree*	*Neutral*	*Total*
	25	1	26
Agri	96.2	3.8	43.3
	44.6	25.0	
	25	3	28
Agri cooli	89.3	10.7	46.7
	44.6	75.0	
	6		6
Others	100		10.0
	10.7		
	56	*4*	*60*
Total	*93.3*	*6.7*	*100*

Chi-square	= 1.49823	Min. E.F.	= .400
D.F.	= 2	Cells with E.F.<5	= 3 of 6 (50.0%)
Significance	= .4728	Number of Missing observations = 0	

Table 4.6C : Attitude of the Women Towards the Statement "Male Children Bring Money to the Family"

Before Experiment—Control Village

Respondents	*Agree*	*Neutral*	*Total*
	18	2	19
Below Rs. 200	89.5	10.5	31.7
	30.4	50.0	
	38	2	40
Rs. 201–Rs. 400	95.0	5.0	66.7
	67.9	50.0	
	56	*4*	*60*
Total	*93.3*	*6.7*	*100*

Chi-square	= .70489	Min. E.F.	= ..067
D.F.	= 2	Cells with E.F.<5	= 4 of 6 (66.7%)
Significance	= .7030	Number of Missing observations = 0	

It is interesting to note here that male members of the community symbolise money. Male members earn dowry. The nature and amount of dowry varies according to the occupation and status of the bridegroom. Even those who do not have any education are given dowry. While the male children are considered an asset to the family, the female children are considered a burden to the parents. The parents of the girls save for the future of the girls, sacrificing their own comforts. The community has certain customs which go against the girls and which are primarily responsible for female infanticide. It is not therefore surprising to see that 90 per cent of the women in the pre-study and 95 per cent of the women in the post-study say that female children are a burden to them. In the post-study also the same trend came to exist.

Table 4.7 : Attitude of the Women Towards the Statement "Female Children are a Burden to the Parents"

Before Experiment—Control Village

Respondents	*Agree*	*Neutral*	*Disagree*	*Total*
Illiterate	32 97.0 59.3	1 3.0 33.3		33 55.0
Semi-literate	22 81.5	2 7.4 40.7	3 11.1 66.7	27 45.0 100
Total	*54* *90.0*	*3* *5.0*	*3* *5.0*	*60* *100*

Chi-square	= 4.63150	Min. E.F.	= 1.350
D.F.	= 2	Cells with E.F.<5=	4 of 6 (66.7%)
Significance	= .0987	No. of Missing observations	= 0

The arrival of the girl child in the family is not generally welcomed by any member of the family. 83.3 per cent of the female population think that one female child is enough for a family (Table 4.8).

The data here show that more than 85 per cent of the female members do not like to have more than one girl-children (Table 4.9).

In Kuppanampatti village, the girl child is considered a burden to the family. This is so because people are not aware of many welfare schemes

Table 4.7A : Attitude of the Women Towards the Statement "Female Children are a Burden to the Parents"

Before Experiment—Control Village

Respondents	*Agree*	*Neutral*	*Disagree*	*Total*
Below Rs. 200	18 94.7 33.3	1 5.3 33.3		19 31.7
Rs.201–Rs.400	35 87.5 64.8	2 5.0 66.7	3 7.5 100	40 66.7
Above Rs.401	1 100 1.9			1 1.7
Total	*54* *90.0*	*3* *5.0*	*3* *5.0*	*60* *100*

Chi-square = 1.63889 Min. E.F. = .050
D.F. = 4 Cells with E.F.<5 = 7 of 9 (77.8%)
Significance = .8018 No. of Missing observations = 0

Table 4.8 : Attitude of the Women Towards the Statement "One Female Child is Enough for a Family"

Before Experiment—Control Village

Respondents	*Agree*	*Neutral*	*Disagree*	*Total*
Below 20	23 82.1 46.0	4 14.3 57.1	1 3.6 33.3	28 46.7
21 to 30	24 88.9 48.0	1 3.7 14.3	2 7.4 66.7	27 45.0
Above 31	3 60.0 6.0	2 40.0 28.6		5 8.3
Total	*50* *83.3*	*7* *11.7*	*3* *5.0*	*60* *100*

Chi-square = 6.18124 Min. E.F. = .250
D.F. = 4 Cells with E.F.<5 = 7 of 9 (77.8%)
Significance = .1860 No. of Missing observations = 0

Table 4.9 : Attitude of the Women Towards the Statement "More than one Girl is a Problem to the Family"

Before Experiment—Control Village

Respondents	*Agree*	*Neutral*	*Disagree*	*Total*
Below 20	24 88.9 46.2	1 3.7 20.0	2 7.4 66.7	27 45.0
21 to 30	24 85.7 46.2	3 10.7 60.0	1 3.6 33.3	28 46.7
Above 31	4 80.0 7.7	1 20.0 20.0		5 8.3
Total	**52** **86.7**	**5** **8.3**	**3** **5.0**	**60** **100**

Chi-square	= 2.42279	Min. E.F.	= .250
D.F.	= 4	Cells with E.F.<5 =	7 of 9 (77.8%)
Significance	= .6585	No. of Missing observations = 0	

for the girl-child, announced by the Government. As a result, women of all age group do not have a positive approach to the problem. The study found that girl children were at a disadvantage when compared with boys. This makes the girl children develop inferiority complex.

In the Indian social context women from childhood are considered a weaker sex who cannot be independent or achieve the goal by themselves. The dependency of women is depicted in various ways in the Hindu social system. Even in the contemporary society, majority of the women in rural and urban areas lack confidence in themselves. The present study shows that 53.3 per cent are of the opinion that women by herself cannot look after a family. Table 4.10 shows that even the younger respondents of Kuppanampatti think that they would not be able to run a family independently.

Literacy, occupation and economic background do not have a say in creating confidence in the family. As shown in Table 4.11 most of the women (68.3 per cent) say that they can run the family even without male support. The trend is very significant that women in large numbers are confident of independently running a family.

Table 4.10 : Attitude of the Women Towards the Statement "A Woman Can Look After a Family"

Before Experiment—Control Village

Respondents	*Agree*	*Neutral*	*Disagree*	*Total*
	8	6	13	27
Below 20	29.6	22.2	48.1	45.0
	50.0	50.0	40.6	
	6	4	18	28
21 to 30	21.4	14.3	64.3	46.7
	37.5	33.3	56.3	
	2	2	1	5
Above 31	40.0	40.0	20.0	8.3
	12.5	16.7	3.1	
	16	*12*	*32*	*60*
Total	*26.7*	*20.0*	*53.3*	*100*

Chi-square = 4.04167 Min. E.F. = 1.000
D.F. = 4 Cells with E.F.<5 = 3 of 9 (33.3%)
Significance = ..4004 No. of Missing observations = 0

Table 4.11 : Attitude of the Women Towards the Statement "A Woman Can Look After a Family only with Male Support"

After Experiment—Control Village

Respondents	*Agree*	*Neutral*	*Disagree*	*Total*
	8	1	19	28
Below 20	28.6	3.6	67.9	46.7
	57.1	20.0	46.3	
	5	2	20	27
21 to 30	18.5	7.4	74.1	45.0
	35.7	40.0	48.8	
	1	2	2	5
Above 31	20.0	40.0	40.0	8.3
	7.1	40.0	40.9	
	14	*5*	*41*	*60*
Total	*23.3*	*8.3*	*68.3*	*100*

Chi-square = 8.14621 Min. E.F. = .417
D.F. = 4 Cells with E.F.<5 = 5 of 9 (55.6%)
Significance = .0864 No. of Missing observations = 0

Here again there can be two reasons. On the one hand, the women among the Thevars were forced to live alone due to several factors. Secondly, ideas developed from modern days might have influenced their minds also. However, the respondents of Kuppanampatti are of the opinion that women cannot do the household job and the income-generation job simultaneously.

The respondents are divided in their opinion when 45 per cent of the women of Kuppanampatti say that it is difficult for women to do outside job and 48.3 per cent of the women say that women can do the jobs simultaneously. The same trend is seen in the post-study also.

The reason for the attitude is that women are not oriented forward taking up any employment. Social dependency forces them not to seek independent employment, unless a good orientation is given, women will not become self-reliant. The women were asked whether they answered the negative in the pre-study and 73.3 per cent of the women expressed negative attitude in the post study also.

It is to be inferred that an interval of six months had changed the attitude. The reason for this also can be attributed to social factors. The customs which are prevailing in the community do not allow the women to go out for a job. Men consider it beneath their dignity to send their women for income-generating jobs, outside home. This attitude of men had influenced women also. This can be attributed to a sense of false prestige.

Moreover, women being the weaker section, believe that they cannot do any job independently.

More than 61.7 per cent of the women are of the opinion that they can do only supportive jobs or part-time jobs. This again shows the dependent nature of women. The respondents think that women who are illiterate, semi-literate or unskilled cannot do any full time work, therefore the women are advised to take up part-time jobs. More over it is a custom for women to be at home when the men return from work. This custom is followed in most of the houses of rural India. Women should receive their husbands or sons and look after them. Therefore 73.3 percent of the women say that their men do not like women going for work. Another reason for not sending their ladies to work is the fear that they may become centre of attraction for other men.

In a society where changes are taking place at a rapid rate there are certain pockets like Kuppanampatti where the change is very slow. Education or economic independence have not reached the village and therefore the women are still traditional in attitude. The women themselves say that the girls need not be given an orientation to take up employment. This attitude is expressed by 31.7 per cent of the women in the pre-study and 33.3 per cent in the post-study (Table 4.12).

Table 4.12 : Attitude of the Women Towards the Statement "Girl Children should be Trained Suitably to Take up an Employment"

After Experiment—Control Village

Respondents	*Agree*	*Neutral*	*Disagree*	*Total*
	13	1	14	28
Below 20	46.4	3.6	50.0	46.7
	34.2	50.0	70.0	
	23		4	27
21 to 30	85.2		14.8	45.0
	60.5		20.0	
	2	1	2	5
Above 31	40.0	20.0	40.0	8.3
	5.3	50.0	10.0	
	38	*2*	*20*	*60*
Total	*63.3*	*3.3*	*33.3*	*100*

Chi-square	= 13.97811	**Min. E.F.**	= .167
D.F.	= 4	**Cells with E.F.<5=**	5 of 9 (55.6%)
Significance	= ..0074	**No. of Missing observations**	= 0

All women irrespective of the background express that girls should not be given an orientation to take up an employment which is very surprising in our modern society. It is essential to change this attitude of women in this context as the number exceeds 25 per cent. It is significant because the attitude-change is possible only if there is a total agreement.

Attitudes towards literacy, self-reliance, the girl child and female infanticide show that women of Kuppanampatti are yet to develop a positive attitude. Women hate themselves because the condition in which they live do not contribute to happiness or peace of mind. In such circumstances, women believe in avoiding female children and so the female infanticide occurs in this village. Most of the respondents in this village support female infanticide due to the prevailing conditions. 51.7% of the women believe that girls should be given equal treatment with boys. This is revealed through Table 4.13.

Table 4.13 : Attitude of the Women Towards the Statement "Girl Children are to be Given Equal Treatment Alongwith the Boys in the Family"

Before Experiment—Control Village

Respondents	*Agree*	*Neutral*	*Disagree*	*Total*
	17	7	3	27
Below 20	63.0	25.9	11.1	45.0
	42.5	46.7	60.0	
	19	7	2	28
21 to 30	67.9	25.0	7.1	46.7
	47.5	46.7	40.0	
	4	1		5
Above 31	80.0	20.0		8.3
	10.0	6.7		
	40	*15*	*5*	*60*
Total	*66.7*	*25*	*8.3*	*100*

Chi-square	= .96839	Min. E.F.	= .417
D.F.	= 4	Cells with E.F.<5 =	5 of 9 (55.6%)
Significance	= ..9146	No. of Missing observations = 0	

93.3 per cent of the women of Kuppanampatti village in the pre-study and 91.7 per cent in the post-study say that the girls should be given extra care (Tables 4.14 and 4.14A).

During adolescence the girls are usually given nutritious food to help their proper growth. Their development, both psychological and physiological, is to be looked after by the parents. Therefore the respondents feel both during adolescence and adulthood the girl should be given full support.

It is interesting to note that the girls are considered a precious commodity once they allow child labour. The girls are not abused or insulted from this stage onwards. The daughter in the family is usually liked by the father, and daughter-in-law is also considered an important person

Table 4.14 : Attitude of the Women Towards the Statement "Girl Children Have to be Given Extra-Care in the Family"

Before Experiment—Control Village

Respondents	*Agree*	*Neutral*	*Disagree*	*Total*
	26	1	1	27
Below 20	96.3	3.7		45.0
	46.4	33.3		
	26	1	1	28.0
21 to 30	92.9	3.6	3.6	46.7
	46.4	33.3	100	
	4	1		5
Above 31	80.0	20.0		8.3
	7.1	33.3		
	56	*3*	*1*	*60*
Total	*93.3*	*50.0*	*1.7*	*100*

Chi-square	= 3.71920	Min. E.F.	= ..083
D.F.	= 4	Cells with E.F.<5 =	7 of 9 (77.8%)
Significance	= .4453	No. of Missing observations = 0	

Table 4.14 A: Attitude of the Women Towards the Statement "Girl Children Have to be Given Extra-Care in the Family"

After Experiment—Control Village

Respondents	*Agree*	*Neutral*	*Disagree*	*Total*
	25	2	1	28
Below 20	89.3	7.1	3.6	46.7
	45.5	66.7	50.0	
	25	1	1	27
21 to 30	92.6	3.7	3.7	45.0
	45.5	33.7	50.0	
	5			5
Above 31	100			8.3
	9.1			
	55	*3*	*2*	*60*
Total	*91.7*	*5.0*	*3.3*	*100*

Chi-square	= .83814	Min. E.F.	= .167
D.F.	= 4	Cells with E.F.<5 =	7 of 9 (77.8%)
Significance	= .9333	No. of Missing observations = 0	

in the family provided there is sound educational background. The respondents feel that there is no opportunity for women to get assaulted or insulted by the members of the family. Around 85 per cent of the women say that girls should never be insulted.

Table 4.15 : Attitude of the Women Towards the Statement "The Girls are not Abused/Insulted"

After Experiment—Control Village

Respondents	*Agree*	*Neutral*	*Disagree*	*Total*
Below 20	24 85.7 47.1	1 3.6 50.0	3 10.7 42.9	28 46.7
21 to 30	23 85.2 45.1	1 3.7 50.0	3 11.1 42.9	27 45.0
Above 31	4 80.0 7.8		1 20.0 14.3	5 8.3
Total	*51* *85.0*	*2* *3.3*	*7* *11.7*	*60* *100*

Chi-square	= .52557	Min. E.F.	= .167
D.F.	= 4	Cells with E.F.<5 =	7 of 9 (77.8%)
Significance	= .9710	No. of Missing observations = 0	

From this one can infer that girls are given affection but it is the circumstances which force them to kill the new-born child.

Thus the female infanticide is sought as a solution from the sufferings of the society. This was the opinion expressed by 55 per cent of the women.

Female infanticide is considered a way-out of social and economic problems. The community which practises female infanticide does not consider its acts to be against religion. 86.7 per cent of the women in the pre study and 88.3 per cent in the post-study say that female infanticide is not against religious practices of their community (Table 4.17 and 4.17A).

Female infanticide is supported by most of the respondents (90%) in Kuppanampatti village. They do not consider it a serious cultural violation, a bad act inviting the wrath of God.

Table 4.16 : Attitude of the Women Towards the Statement "It is Better to Kill the Child as soon as it is Born Instead of Allowing it to Face Problems Throughout Life"

Before Experiment—Control Village

Respondents	*Agree*	*Neutral*	*Disagree*	*Total*
Below 20	15 55.6 45.5	7 25.9 41.2	5 18.5 50.0	27 45.0
21 to 30	15 53.6 45.5	9 32.1 52.9	4 14.3 40.0	28 46.7
Above 31	3 60.0 9.1	1 20.0 5.9	1 20.0 10.0	5 8.3
Total	*33* *55.0*	*17* *28.3*	*10* *16.7*	*60* *100*

Chi-square = .53995 Min. E.F. = .833
D.F. = 4 Cells with E.F.<5 = 5 of 9 (55.6%)
Significance = .9695 No. of Missing observations = 0

Table 4.16A : Attitude of the Women Towards the Statement "It is Better to Kill the Child as soon as it is Born Instead of Allowing it to Face Problems Throughout Life"

After Experiment—Control Village

Respondents	*Agree*	*Neutral*	*Disagree*	*Total*
Below 20	19 67.9 41.3	5 17.9 62.5	4 14.3 66.7	28 46.7
21 to 30	24 88.9 52.2	1 3.7 12.5	2 7.4 33.3	27 45.0
Above 31	3 60.0 6.5	2 40.0 25.0		5 8.3
Total	*46* *76.7*	*8* *13.3*	*6* *10.0*	*60* *100*

Chi-square = 7.16066 Min. E.F. = .500
D.F. = 4 Cells with E.F.<5 = 7 of 9 (77.8%)
Significance = .1276 No. of Missing observations = 0

Table 4.17: Attitude of the Women Towards the Statement "Female Infanticide is Against Religion"

Before Experiment—Control Village

Respondents	*Agree*	*Neutral*	*Disagree*	*Total*
	2	4	21	27
Below 20	7.4	14.8	77.8	45.0
	100	66.7	40.4	
		1	27	28
21 to 30		3.6	96.4	46.7
		16.7	51.9	
		1	4	5
Above 31		20.0	80.0	8.3
		16.7	7.7	
	2	*6*	*52*	*60*
Total	*3.3*	*10.0*	*86.7*	*100*

Chi-square = 5.30718 Min. E.F. = .167
D.F. = 4 Cells with E.F.<5 = 7 of 9 (77.8%)
Significance = .2572 No. of Missing observations = 0

Table 4.17 A: Attitude of the Women Towards the Statement "Female Infanticide is Against Religion"

After Experiment—Control Village

Respondents	*Agree*	*Neutral*	*Disagree*	*Total*
	3		25	28
Below 20	10.7		89.3	46.7
	50.0		47.2	
	3		24	27
21 to 30	11.1		88.9	45.0
	50.0		45.3	
		1	4	5
Above 31		20.0	80.0	8.3
		100	7.5	
	6	*1*	*53*	*60*
Total	*10.0*	*1.7*	*88.3*	*100*

Chi-square = 11.59075 Min. E.F. = .083
D.F. = 4 Cells with E.F.<5 = 7 of 9 (77.8%)
Significance = .0207 No. of Missing observations = 0

5

Adult Education as a Solution for Female Infanticide

Introducation

Education is a prerequisite for development. It endows people with knowledge, skills and purpose. In broad terms, education is a socialization process, which facilitates not only learning but shapes also modes of behaviour and thinking. India, like other developing countries, gives high priority to education, as an instrument and facilitator of the developing process.[1]

In the history of mankind, education formed the major basis for the development of the human society. Through the development of attitude and values, capabilities and skills emerge Education. This provides strength and resilience to people to respond to changing situations. It enables them to contribute to society's development. History has established beyond doubt the crucial role played by resources which is the main function of education.[2]

To achieve the multiple but interdependent goals of personal, economic, political and cultural development, it is necessary to make an appropriate provision for integrated programmes of education for people, who are at difference levels of personal and economic development, possessing different linguistic, social and cultural backgrounds. Such programmes should have curricula suitable for the categories, which would strengthen the unity within diversity and also facilitate mobility from one part of the country another.

To enable the education system to play its role effectively in the process of national development, along democratic lines, the benefit of education should reach all levels of people.

Education for values has acquired a new dimension and a new urgency in India. We are, trying to fulfil two formidable tasks, namely, achieving quality-contest transformation and broad basing education to meet the emerging needs of tomorrow.

Indian Adult Education Scenario

Indian Education system provides types of educational facilities at different levels, we have education at the elementary non-formal/adult, higher, technical, and management levels, besides distance education. It seems essential to juxtapose he scenario of the education system against the internal dynamics of a society, in which 64 per cent of the population is illiterate and most of them are living in the rural areas. In this context, we could pay more attention to the adult, non-formal education and distance system for raising the levels of functional literacy, which would be divided into two strategies of education, like

- Adult Education for the age group : 15–35
- Distance Education for all age groups.

The ancient scriptures of India define education as that which liberates i.e., provides the instrument for liberation from ignorance and oppression. In the modern world, it would naturally include the ability to read and write. Adult education, which aims at adult functional/development literacy, thus assumes great significance in a country of illiterates.

Along with the expansion of facilities for formal education, tremendous efforts are being made to spread literacy through various adult education programmes. All available resources are being mobilised to achieve the goal of universal literacy and education as rapidly as possible.

Mahatma Gandhi, the Father of the Nation, considered illiteracy to be India's sin and shame. The situation continues to be alarming in absolute terms. There were 437 million illiterates in 1981 compared with approximately 300 million in 1948 when Indian attained Independence. It is nevertheless true, that there has been progress in literacy also. Literates who accounted for only 16.67 per cent in 1951, became 36.23 per cent in 1981.

Undoubtedly efforts in the field of elementary education and adult education programmes are negated by a high rate of growth of population. This, however underlines the need for a more decisive action particularly leading to the acceptance of planning practices. If we assume that there is no change in population and the rate of growth of literacy, then there would be 500 million illiterates in India in the year 2,000 A.D. According to the World Bank, in that year 54 per cent of the World's illiterate population in the age group 15-19, would be in India (Challenge of Education, a Policy Perspective, 1985).

Adult Education

Adult education, as is clear from the name, implies education of adults, mainly those who could not get any formal education in their early days. "Adult education may be defined broadly as to include all instruction, formal or informal, imparted to adults. Literacy and citizenship are its two main ingredients. "Adult education may be concerned with any or more of these aspects of an individual's life - his work life, his personal life or his life as a citizen".[3] In India adult education has two aspects:

a) Adult literacy, i.e., education of those adults who never had any schooling.

b) Continuing education of the adult literate".[4]

Adult education is increasingly being seen in its totality, Liveright and Haygood declared that "Adult education is the process whereby person who no longer (or did not) attend school on a regular and full time basis undertake sequential and organised activities with the conscious intention of bringing about changes in information, knowledge, understanding or skills, appreciation and attitudes, or for the purpose of identifying and solving personal or community problems".[5]

UNESCO defines a literate person as one "one can with understanding both read and write a short simple statement in his every day life".[6] A person is functionally literate when he can "engage in all those activities in which literacy is required for effective functioning of his group and community".[7]

National Objectives of Adult Education

i) To provide functional literacy education for adults for who have never had the advantage of any formal education.

ii) To provide functional remedial education for those young people who prematurely dropped out of the formal school system.

iii) To provide further education for different categories who complete the formal education system in order to improve their basic knowledge and skills.

iv) To provide in-service, on-the-job, vocational and professionals training.

v) To give the adult citizen of the country the necessary aesthetic, cultural and civic education for public enlightenment.[8]

Adult Education in India

The concept of adult education was mainly confined to literacy in the pre-Independence period. The first five year plan of India found it too narrow to be able to meet the various needs of the adults in the changed socio-political conditions obtaining in free India. It was, therefore, widened to include, in addition to literacy, health, recreation, home-life of the adults, and their economic life and citizenship training; and to denote this new concept, the term social education was coined.[9] It implied an all comprehensive programme of community uplift through community action.

A second land mark in the development of the concept of adult education in India came in 1978, when adult education was made a part of the revised minimum needs programme. In view of their implications for the family and the society in general, literacy and adult education among women, particularly in rural areas, was to be promoted through special efforts.

The Sixth Five Year Plan made very specific comment in this regard. The NAEP (National Adult Education Programme) was not meant to remove illiteracy alone, but also to impart functional education and create awareness among the learners about social problems. Adult education thus includes measures for continuing education to sustain the interests of those adults who have taken advantage of it and to enable them to upgrade their knowledge and skills on their own.

The Seventh Plan found that the existing education system widely failed in its content and process in relation to the requirements of the country. In 1990 attempts were made to cover all adult illiterates in the age group 15-35 years. All developmental programmes, especially those affecting the rural and the urban poor were required to include a component of adult education and literacy aimed at the needs of the beneficiaries of development programmes. To promote motivation among adult learners appropriate and effective programmes of post-literacy were to be developed with adequate linkages to work and further education.[10]

A National Literacy Mission was launched in May 1988 to eliminate illiteracy by 1995 positively.[11]

Adult Education in Tamil Nadu

In 1978, a mass programme of functional literacy popularly known as "National Adult Education Programme" (NAEP) was launched. However, this programme failed to deliver the goods as expected.

In 1986, the Mass Programme of Functional Literacy (MPFL) was launched providing for the involvement of the schools and colleges, as the students were expected to have plenty of voluntarism and take up teaching with great eagerness. There was only a mild response.

The defects in NAEP were enumerated and a new plan of action under the name of the National Literacy Mission (NLM) was launched in 1988. There was an overall improvement in the rate of coverage but it was still much below the targeted figures.

Literacy campaign in the eight districts in Tamil Nadu has helped the brand of seekers of a new path. A popular slogan is now heard in every nook and corner of the villages in Tamil Nadu, "Karpom Karppippom", meaning "Let us learn! Let us teach!

The first candle of TLC was lit in Sivaganga, then in Pasumpon Muthuramalingam District, in April 1991, followed by Kamaraja and Pundukkottai Districts.

Madurai District, initiated the literacy campaign in November 1991 with a target of 4.20 lakhs to be made literate by November 1992.

Adult Education for Women

Education is an indispensable component of human resource development. In a developing country, the contribution of woman is as indispensable as that of man. Every woman of the nation expected to play her role inside and outside the home. Women bear most of the burden and they are yet not recognised for their contribution. Their performance is being given low status and low pay. Most of the women are poorly equipped, as their educational level is very low. They are less equipped to make decisions as their educational level is very low.

The India Government therefore decided to impart education to women and it started an adult education programme for adult illiterates from October 2, 1978 all over the country. Women are greatly interested in learning to balance their home budgets. So they like such types of education which help them in increasing their income. Tailoring, knitting and embroidery work, cooking, basket-making, artificial flower-making and making fancy things are some of the skills they are eager to learn, as these would contribute to extra income.

The present democratic system of the country gives equal rights to each individual. But the reality is that due to ignorance, many illiterate women are unable to exercise properly their rights at the time of elections. Most of the illiterate women often are influenced by superstitions and many other social evils. With proper education these women will get rid of superstitions, caste feelings, inferiority complex etc. Adult education programme for women should not be confined to literacy education only. Women have to be empowered, through knowledge so that they are not exploited. Adult education is a developmental programme. It is, therefore essential that grass-root beneficiaries should be associated with the planning and implementation of the programme. Awareness-building in the present state of society is a task which adult educators must perform with a sense of mission, commitment and dedication. Adult Education programmes must consist of :

a) a basic course of functional literacy which will include skills of reading, writing and arithmetic, simple techniques of home management, information on human relationship, nutrition, health and child care.

b) a course of liberal education which may be covered in three or four stages.

c) vocational or professional courses at different levels.

Adult education for women necessitates consideration of many dimensions. It is not just literacy drives directed towards women, but making the total programme conducive to generating positive appreciation of the status, the role and the functions of women in the society, both at the macro and at the micro levels.

Women and Literacy

A low rate of female literacy in Indian has always been a matter of concern. In Uttar Pradesh, India's most populous state, female literacy at 26.02 per cent has trailed behind the male literacy rate of 55.35 per cent. In Rajasthan, India's desert state, the percentage of women's literacy is even lower, that is, 20.84 against 55.07 for men. The state of Kerala is the only exception where female literacy record is an high as 86.93 per cent against male literacy rate of 94.95 per cent. The national average of female literacy (1991 census) is only 39.42 per cent while the average male literacy rate stands at 63.86 per cent.

Female illiteracy in India can be attributed to several economic and social compulsions. The tragic necessity to send out the girl child as a domestic help or a baby-sitter to bring in extra-needed money stands in the way of female literacy. Socially, Gender inequality has had a long innings in India. While a male child is looked upon as an augmenter of the family's income, a female child is looked upon as a drain on the family's resources. As a result, while boys receive a great deal of affection, girls tend to receive very little of everything.

In addition to such discriminatory attitudes, the paucity of neighbourhood schools to which girls could be sent has also affected the rate of female literacy.

A Change in the Attitudes

These, and other reasons have hindered the growth of female literacy until recently though, old hangovers still persist in varying degrees. Now a change is discernible in people's attitudes. New employment opportunities for girls are opening up in all fields, enabling them to make their mark as income-earners instead of being mere 'doers' of domestic chores. Besides, literacy among women is widely known to have a strong impact on child-bearing. Literate women tend to marry late and also tend to be well-informed about family planning.

Moreover, indicators of socio-economic development and the physical quality of life index in several sociological studies have clearly brought out the relevance of literacy and education of women to the needs of the present-day society. The National Policy of Education has assigned an emphatic, interventionist role to education for bringing about change in the status in women.

Once women start perceiving the relevance of education, they will send their children, especially girls, to school. The prevention of child marriage, matters relating to maternity, hygiene and sanitation have begun to engage the attention of women.

Today, classes for women, comprising not more than thirty learners each, are run by women only, preferably at mid-day, after the morning chores are done. Women are allowed to bring their young children and babies to the class room, while young girls are allowed to bring their wards along with them.

The lessons in their primers are so designed that learning to read and write goes along with learning to be good mothers and homemakers. A class begins with a literacy song sung by all the participants. Frequently, in between lessons, the class teacher invites knowledgeable people both men and women to come and speak to the learners on topics that range from nutrition to child care, pregnancy, the control of family size or any other subject, according to their choice.

To enliven the learning hour and awaken their latent talents learners are encouraged to organise mimicry shows, short skits and chorus singing, all carrying an exhortation to women to become literate and learn skills to build a better tomorrow for their children and society.

Notes :

1. A Muthumanickam, "Study of Selected Rural Television Forums with regard to Knowledge and Attitude Levels of the Learners', Unpublished Ph.D. thesis, University of Madras, 1993, p.1.
2. *Ibid.*, p.2.
3. K.K. Bhatia, et. al., *Contemporary Problems of Indian Education*, 1981, p. 214.

4. *Ibid.*
5. C.L. Kundu, *Adult Education*, 1984, p.2.
6. "Literacy : A Peoples Movement", *National Literacy Mission*, 1992, p.4.
7. *Ibid.*
8. C.L. Kundu, *op. cit.*, p. 3.
9. Sita Ram Sharma, *Development of Adult Education in India*, p.254.
10. *Ibid.*, p. 258.
11. *Ibid.*, p. 259.

6

Impact of Adult Education on Women's Attitude Towards Female Infanticide

An experiment was conducted to assess the attitude-change among the women of Usilampatti taluk. This was done primarily to know the impact of adult education as a medium of change. It is assumed that adult education has an impact on the attitude of adults. In order to know this two villages were selected from the same area namely Kuppanampatti and Nadumuthalaikulam, where Kuppanampatti is treated as control village, and Nadumuthalaikulam as an experimental village. In the experimental village an adult education programme was conducted for six months dividing the respondents into two categories of 30 women each.

In the previous chapter the results of the control village namely Kuppanampatti has been given in detail. It is to be noted here that the attitude towards women was studied using four parameters namely women's attitude towards literacy, women's attitude towards the girl-child, women's attitude towards self reliance and their attitude towards female infanticide. In the control village the results of the pre-study and the post-study did not have much variation and the attitude remained more or less the same throughout six months. Whatever the changes that were seen in the control village were due to some external factors beyond the control of the investigation. The results of the study in the control village shows that the attitude towards women was not encouraging in this area. The respondents had a negative attitude towards literacy, girl-child, self reliance but a positive attitude towards female infanticide. All the four factors chosen for the study are important for the personality-development of the women. It is in this context that it was decided to change the attitude of the women towards the better development of the personality. In rural societies the progress can be achieved only through making the society became aware of economic improvement, the need for education etc. This is possible mainly by educating the rural folk.

One of the main signs of a society's development is women's development. A society can be said to be developed only if that society's women register progress. Therefore any adverse development in this category would only indicate the degeneration of the society. Female infanticide occurring in this area indicates the level of social development and the society's attitude to women. In order to eliminate female infanticide an attitudinal change through education is essential. An adult education programme therefore was introduced in Nadumuthalaikulam, is given in Nadumuthalaikulam.

After concluding the first study an adult education kit was prepared taking into consideration the socio-economic background of the village. The 60 respondents were assigned to two adult education centres and they were given lessons regularly. The kit included audio cassettes, video cassettes and several other programmes suitable to the environment. After giving through instructions for 6 months, attitude was measured again. There was a considerable difference in the attitude and thus adult education proved to be a successful programme in the village.

In the village (Experimental—Nadumuthalaikulam) mean during the first study was 4.97 and after the study the mean was 19.90 (Appendix III) whereas in the second study the sample mean was 6.67 and 19.40 (Appendix IV) respectively. From the mean value it can be inferred that women of Nadumuthalaikulam had a positive attitude towards literacy and they were keen on education because they became aware of the fact that education could change society. 8.3 per cent of the women in the pre-study and 96.7 per cent in the post-study said that education was necessary for every day life. Many instances were cited to show that education had helped the people in carrying out their day-today work. Women were made to realise that education would change the outlook on life. Thus a large number of women became aware of the need for education except two married semi-literates who were agriculturalists.

Table 6.1 : Attitude of the Women Towards the Statement "Education is Necessary for Every Day Life"

Before Experiment—Experimental Village

Respondents	*Agree*	*Neutral*	*Disagree*	*Total*
Below 20	2 8.3 40.0	1 4.2 33.3	21 87.5 40.4	24 40.0
21 to 30	3 9.1 60.0	2 6.1 66.7	28 84.8 53.8	33 55.0
Above 31			3 100 5.8	3 5.0
Total	*5* *8.3*	*3* *5.0*	*52* *86.7*	*60* *100*

Chi-square = .60635 Min. E.F. = .150
D.F. = 4 Cells with E.F.<5 = 7 of 9 (77.8%)
Significance = .9624 No. of Missing observations = 0

Table 6.1 A : Attitude of the Women Towards the Statement "Education is Necessary for Every Day Life"

After Experiment—Experimental Village

Respondents	*Necessary*	*Neutral*	*Total*
Below 20	23 95.8 39.7	1 4.2 50.0	24 40.0
21 to 30	32 97.0 55.2	1 3.0 50.0	33 55.0
Above 31	3 100.0 5.2		3 5.0
Total	*58* *96.7*	*2* *3.3*	*60* *100*

Chi-square = .16458 Min. E.F. = .100
D.F. = 2 Cells with E.F.<5 = 4 of 6 (66.7%)
Significance = .9210 No. of Missing observations = 0

Table 6.1 B : Attitude of the Women Towards the Statement "Education is Necessary for Every Day Life"

After Experiment—Experimental Village

Respondents	*Necessary*	*Neutral*	*Total*
Illiterate	36 100 62.1		36 60
Semi-Literate	22 91.7 37.9	2 8.3 100	24 40.0
Total	*58* *96.7*	*2* *3.3*	*60* *100*

Chi-square = 1.05603 3.10345 Min. E.F. = .800
D.F. = 1 1 Cells with E.F.<5 = 2 of 4 (50.0%)
Significance = .3041 .0781 (Before Yates
No. of Missing observations = 0 Correlation

Table 6.1 C : Attitude of the Women Towards the Statement "Education is Necessary for Every Day Life"

After Experiment—Experimental Village

Respondents	*Necessary*	*Neutral*	*Total*
Agri	23 92.0 39.7	2 8.0 100.0	25 41.7
Agri Cooli	28 100 48.3		28 46.7
Others	7 100.0 12.1		7 11.7
Total	*58* *96.7*	*2* *3.3*	*60* *100*

Chi-square = 2.89655 Min. E.F. = .233
D.F. = 2 Cells with E.F.<5 = 3 of 6 (50.0%)
Significance = .2350 No. of Missing observations = 0

Table 6.1 D : Attitude of the Women Towards the Statement "Education is Necessary for Every Day Life"

After Experiment—Experimental Village

Respondents	*Necessary*	*Neutral*	*Total*
Below Rs.200	47 95.9 81.0	2 4.1 100.0	49 81.7
Rs. 201 to 400	11 100 19.0		11 18.3
Total	*58* *96.7*	*2* *3.3*	*60* *100*

Chi-square = .0000 .46446
D.F. = 1 1
Significance = 1.000 .4955
No. of Missing observations = 0

Min. E.F. = .367
Cells with E.F.<5 = 2 of 4 (50.0%)
(Before Yates
Correlation

Table 6.1 E : Attitude of the Women Towards the Statement "Education is Necessary for Every Day Life"

After Experiment—-Experimental Village

Respondents	*Necessary*	*Neutral*	*Total*
Married	53 96.4 91.4	2 3.6 100	55 91.7
Unmarried	5 100 8.6		5 8.3
Total	*58* *96.7*	*2* *3.3*	*60* *100*

Chi-square = .0000 .18809
D.F. = 1 1
Significance = 1.000 .6645
No. of Missing observations = 0

Min. E.F. = .167
Cells with E.F.<5 = 3 of 4 (75.0%)
(Before Yates
Correlation

In the pre-study only 3.3 per cent of the women were having positive attitude towards education. In the post-study 88.3 per cent of the women revealed a negative attitude towards education. Due to the impact of adult education women became confident that learning the 3 R's will help them in education.

They felt that reading the writing will help in broadening their ideas and attitude. Thus when 50 per cent of the women respondents were neutral in the pre-study regarding literacy 98.3 per cent in the post study agreed that literacy would help them in education. Only one women had a neutral attitude towards literacy after the experiment.

Table 6.2 : Attitude of the Women Towards the Statement "Literacy Will Help the Education"

Before Experiment—Experimental Village

Respondents	*Agree* 1	*Neutral* 2	*Disagree* 3	*Total*
	2	10	12	24
Below 20	8.3	41.7	50.0	40.0
	100	33.3	42.9	
		18	15	33
21 to 30		54.5	45.5	55.0
		60.0	53.6	
		2	1	3
Above 31		66.7	33.3	5.0
		6.7	3.6	
	2	*30*	*28*	*60*
Total	*3.3*	*50.0*	*46.7*	*100*

Chi-square	= 3.81819	Min. E.F.	= .100
D.F.	= 4	Cells with E.F.<5	= 5 of 9 (55.6%)
Significance	= .4312	No. of Missing observations	= 0

When they became fully aware of the importance of education they felt that they did not get education at the proper time. Many respondents were illiterate or semi-literate because they were not sent to school. When the adult education programme was given they became interested in knowing about school education. In the pre-study in Nadumuthalaikulam 35 per cent of the respondents agreed that school education was not necessary for progress and 53.3 per cent of the women respondents said

Table 6.2 A : Attitude of the Women Towards the Statement "Literacy Will Help the Education"

After Experiment—Experimental Village

Respondents	*Agree* 1	*Neutral* 2	*Total*
	23	1	24
Below 20	95.0	4.2	40.0
	39.0	100	
	33		33
21 to 30	100		55.0
	55.9		
	3		3
Above 31	100		5.0
	5.1		
	59	*1*	*60*
Total	*98.3*	*1.7*	*100*

Chi-square = 1.52542 Min. E.F. = .050
D.F. = 2 Cells with E.F.<5 = 4 of 6 (66.7%)
Significance = .4664 No. of Missing observations = 0

Table 6.2 B : Attitude of the Women Towards the Statement "Literacy Will Help the Education"

After Experiment—Experimental Village

Respondents	*Essential* 1	*Neutral* 2	*Not Essential* 3	*Total*
	2	3	19	24
Below 20	8.3	12.5	79.2	40.0
	100	60.0	35.8	
		2	31	33
21 to 30		6.1	93.9	55.0
		40.0	58.5	
			3	3
Above 31			100	5.0
			5.7	
	2	*5*	*53*	*60*
Total	*3.3*	*8.3*	*88.3*	*100*

Chi-square = 4.34648 Min. E.F. = .100
D.F. = 4 Cells with E.F.<5 = 7 of 9 (77.8%)
Significance = .3611 No. of Missing observations = 0

that school education was not necessary for progress.

Table 6.3 : Attitude of the Women Towards the Statement "School Education is Necessary for Progress"

Before Experiment—Experimental Village

Respondents	*Agree*	*Neutral*	*Disagree*	*Total*
Below 20	10 41.7 47.6	3 12.5 42.9	11 45.8 34.4	24 40.0
21 to 30	9 27.3 42.9	3 9.1 42.9	21 63.6 65.6	33 55.0
Above 31	2 66.7 9.5	1 33.3 14.3		3 5.0
Total	*21* *35.0*	*7* *11.7*	*32* *53.3*	*60* *100*

Chi-square	= 5.64631	Min. E.F.	= .350
D.F.	= 4	Cells with E.F.<5 =	5 of 9 (55.6%)
Significance	= .2272	No. of Missing observations = 0	

Table 6.3 A : Attitude of the Women Towards the Statement "School Education is Necessary for Progress"

After Experiment—Experimental Village

Respondents	*Agree*	*Neutral*	*Disagree*	*Total*
Illiterate	19 79.2	1 4.2	4 16.7	24 40.0
Semi	31 93.9 58.5	2	33 6.1 33.3	55.0
Above 31	3 100 5.7			3 5.0
Total	*53* *88.3*	*1* *1.7*	*6* *10.0*	*60* *100*

Chi-square	= 3.77073	Min. E.F.	= .050
D.F.	= 4	Cells with E.F.<5 =	7 of 9 (77.8%)
Significance	= .4379	No. of Missing observations = 0	

In the post-study the investigation found out that 88.3 per cent women's attitude was changed regarding school education. After 6 months of the adult education the women believe that early education is better than adult education and school can provide necessary education for eradicating the women illiteracy which is a big problem in the rural areas.

But many women are still undecided about sending their children to school. It is only in Nadumuthalaikulam, due to the impact of adult education the women have become aware of the benefits of education. So they decided to send their children for a few years to school. But even in the post-study 60 per cent of the women were not satisfied with five years of schooling or primary education. The women respondents want to send their children to the secondary and high school levels. They want to become literate as quick as possible.

Table 6.4 : Attitude of the Women Towards the Statement "Minimum of Five Years of Education in School is Necessary to Eradicate Illiteracy"

After Experiment—Experimental Village

Respondents	*Agree*	*Neutral*	*Disagree*	*Total*
	8	4	12	24
Below 20	33.3	16.7	50.0	40.0
	47.1	57.1	33.3	
	7	3	23	33
21 to 30	21.2	9.1	69.7	55.0
	41.2	42.9	63.9	
	2		1	3
Above 31	66.7		33.3	5.0
	11.8		2.8	
	17	*7*	*36*	*60*
Total	*28.3*	*11.7*	*60.0*	*100*

Chi-square	= 4.6829	Min. E.F.	= .350
D.F.	= 4	Cells with E.F.<5 =	5 of 9 (55.6%)
Significance	= .3214	No. of Missing observations = 0	

The result of this study shows that all women respondents would become literate, provided they are given an opportunity. This attitudinal change was very significant because in the pre-study 78.3 per cent of the women that they did not want to become literate. The impact of adult education was so great that all the respondents wanted to be literate.

Table 6.5 : Attitude of the Women Towards the Statement "Given an Opportunity Will You Become Literate ?"

Before Experiment—Experimental Village

Respondents	*Sure* 1	*Neutral* 2	*Never* 3	*Total*
Below 20	2 8.3 50.0	4 16.7 54.4	18 75.0 38.3	24 40.0
21 to 30	2 6.1 50.0	5 15.2 55.6	26 78.8 55.3	33 55.0
Above 31			3 100 6.4	3 5.0
Total	*4* *6.7*	*9* *15.0*	*47* *78.3*	*60* *100*

Chi-square	= 1.02783	Min. E.F.	= .200
D.F.	= 4	Cells with E.F.<5 =	7 of 9 (77.8%)
Significance	= .9055	No. of Missing observations = 0	

As the women respondents became more and more interested in education they started giving equal importance to sending boys and girls to school. Formerly the rural society believed that education was necessary only for boys. As a result of this in the pre-study 23.3 per cent of the respondents felt that education was necessary only for boys whereas in the pre-study only 6.7 per cent gave this opinion.

Thus change in the attitude is very clear. In order to support this statement the investigator asked the question whether education was necessary for girls. In the pre-study 11.7 per cent gave an affirmative answer (Table 6.6) whereas in the post-study 98.3) per cent gave an affirmative answer (Table 6.6A). One women had a negative attitude towards sending girls for education. This respondent is illiterate but has a sound agricultural background.

From the analysis given above one can see the difference in attitude

Table 6.6 : Attitude of the Women Towards the Statement "Education is Necessary for Girls Too"

Before Experiment—Experimental Village

Respondents	*Agree*	*Neutral*	*Disagree*	*Total*
Below 20	2 8.3 28.6	4 16.7 36.4	18 75.0 45.9	24 40.0
21 to 30	4 12.1 57.1	7 21.2 63.3	22 66.7 52.4	33 55.0
Above 31	1 33.3 14.3		2 66.7 4.8	3 5.0
Total	*7* *11.7*	*11* *18.3*	*42* *70.0*	*60* *100*

Chi-square = 2.31995 Min. E.F. = .350
D.F. = 4 Cells with E.F.<5 = 6 of 9 (66.7%)
Significance = .6771 No. of Missing observations = 0

Table 6.6 A : Attitude of the Women Towards the Statement "Education is Necessary for Girls Too"

After Experiment—Experimental Village

Respondents	*Agree*	*Neutral*	*Total*
Below 20	24 100 40.7		24 40.0
21 to 30	32 97.0 54.2	1 3.0 100	33 55.0
Above 31	3 100 5.1		3 5.0
Total	*59* *98.3*	*1* *1.7*	*60* *100*

Chi-square = .833205 Min. E.F. = .050
D.F. = 2 Cells with E.F.<5 = 4 of 6 (66.7%)
Significance = .6597 No. of Missing observations = 0

before and after the test towards education. One of the characteristic features of the rural society is the economic structure. A person with good economic background stands higher than a person with sound education. The rural society gives much importance to economic ranking than educational ranking. Here it is clear that many respondents are of the opinion that education is not necessary if the economic background of the individual is sound. Thus the attitudinal change in this regard is also very gradual. Though economy and education were differentiated by the women of Nadumuthalaikulam there was a significant impact of adult education on the relationship of education and married life.

In the pre-study only 20 per cent of the women said that education would help them in leading a happy married life whereas in the post-study 98.3 per cent said that education could lead to a happy married life. Along with this they agreed that education was necessary to face the calamities of life.

Here also after the experiment 98.3 per cent of he women respondents emphasized a negative correlation as far as education and calamities of life were concerned. This may be due to the fact that the adult education kit included matters relating to the evils of dowry and the eradication of dowry. Thus almost all the women know about the importance of education after the introduction of adult education programme. Making an impact, adult education provide to be one of the good tools. It is after the introduction of adult education, the attitude of the women respondents changed towards education.

The adult education can change not only the attitude towards education but also the attitude towards the girl-child. Here the experiment continued and a change was brought about in the attitude towards the girl-child. The Indian society considered the girls to be inferior due to several social factors and one of the important factors is that according to the Hindu belief, the parents will go to heaven only if the sons lit the funeral pyre. This is a strong belief that exists among the Hindus which accords a lower status to the girls. The present study changed the attitude of women in this regard also.

In pre-study when 85 per-cent said that the boys were essential to perform the funeral rites, (Table 6.7) in the post-study only 33.3 per cent gave this answer (Table 6.7 A). The adult education showed that even the

Table 6.7 : Attitude of the Women Towards the Statement "A Boy is Essential to Light the Funeral Pyre"
Before Experiment—Experimental Village

Respondents	*Essential*	*Not Essential*	*Total*
Below 20	18 75.0 35.3	6 25.0 66.7	24 40.0
21 to 30	31 93.9 60.8	2 6.1 22.2	33 55.0
Above 31	2 66.7 3.9	1 33.3 11.1	3 5.0
Total	*51* *85.0*	*9* *15.0*	*60* *100*

Chi-square = 4.74153 Min. E.F. = .450
D.F. = 2 Cells with E.F.<5 = 4 of 6 (66.7%)
Significance = .0934 No. of Missing observations = 0

Table 6.7 A : Attitude of the Women Towards the Statement "A Boy is Essential to Light the Funeral Pyre"
After Experiment—Experimental Village

Respondents	*Agree*	*Neutral*	*Not Essential*	*Total*
Below 20	10 41.7 50.0		14 58.3 35.9	24 40.0
21 to 30	8 24.2 40.0	1 3.0 100	24 72.7 61.5	33 35.0
Above 31	2 66.7 10.0		1 33.3 2.6	3 5.0
Total	*20* *33.3*	*1* *1.7*	*39* *65.0*	*60* *100*

Chi-square = 4.06643 Min. E.F. = .050
D.F. = 4 Cells with E.F.<5 = 5 of 9 (55.6%)
Significance = .3971 No. of Missing observations = 0

girls can light the funeral pyre and as a result of that, many literate women had changed their attitudes in the post-study. Usually if there are only female children the funeral pyre could be lit by some one having a son-like relationship of the deceased. However in this community in exceptional cases funeral pyre could be lit by girls also. Thus in the pre-study as well as in the post-study the respondents felt that the girls could be allowed to light the funeral pyre. In the post-study the number of respondents who felt like this increased considerably.

Though the experiment was a successful one the six months programme of adult education was not able to bring a total change in the attitude of women. In the experimental village the first study conducted showed 85 per cent of the women as saying that female children were a problem to the family. In the post-study 35 per cent gave the same answer. Thus the study was able to change the attitude of 50 per cent of the population. The social factors were so strong that even education could not free a female child completely.

The educated girls are given in marriage after the payment of dowry. Though the women respondents in this village agreed that education could change the personality, they were not sure that this would help maintain their economic standard. Women respondents were of the opinion that the problem of dowry could not be removed through education. Thus the women respondents felt that even educated girls were a burden to the family. At the same time the opinion was the reverse as far as the boys were concerned. The educated women of the experimental village say that boys are an asset to the family as they bring money to the family. 53.3 per cent of the respondents after the experiment felt the same way.

The parents consider female child as a burden because economically as well as socially they pose problem to parents. The present study was able to change this attitude to a certain extent. In the pre-study 85 per cent of the women said the girls were a burden to the parents whereas in the post-study 26.7 per cent only said that they were a burden to the parents.

Many parents even today feel that one female child is enough for a family. This view was expressed by 76.7 per cent of the women respondents in the post-study.

In the pre-study the number was considerably less as it was only 11.7 per cent.

It is interesting to note that certain aspects cannot be changed even through education. This study was not able to change the attitude regarding the number of girls in the family. In Nadumuthalaikulam, which is the experiment village, the pre-study and the post-study reveal that a girl-child is not favoured by the women respondents.

In the pre-study 73.3 per cent said that more than one girl was bad for the family (Table 6.8), whereas in the post-study 81.7 per cent said the same (Table 6.8.A). The impact of adult education is found only on literacy and not on the girl-child. When the adult education programme was able to make an impact, the attitude of women to literacy was not able to change the attitude towards the girl-child. This may be due to the fact that though they are well aware that they can change the personality through education, the society around them is not changed. Therefore the status of women remained the same. The adult education programme may be having a long-term impact rather than short-term impact. Immediate change is questionable in this phenomenon which is seen here when the study shows difference in the attitudes towards literacy and the girl-child.

Table 6.8 : Attitude of the Women Towards the Statement "More than one Girl is a Problem to the Family"

Before Experiment—Experimental Village

Respondents	*Agree*	*Neutral*	*Disagree*	*Total*
	16		8	24
Below 20	66.7		33.3	40.0
	36.4		57.1	
	26	1	6	33
21 to 30	78.8	3.0	18.2	55.0
	59.1	50.0	42.9	
	2	1		3
Above 31	66.7	33.3		5.0
	4.5	50.0		
	44	*2*	*14*	*60*
Total	*73.3*	*3.3*	*23.3*	*100*

Chi-square	= .64675	Min. E.F.	= .1333
D.F.	= 2	Cells with E.F.<5 =	3 of 6 (50.0%)
Significance	= .7237	No. of Missing observations = 0	

Table 6.8 A : Attitude of the Women Towards the Statement "More than One Girl is a Problem to the Family"

After Experiment—Experimental Village

Respondents	*Agree*	*Disagree*	*Total*
Below 20	17 70.8 34.7	7 29.2 63.6	24 40.0
21 to 30	29 87.9 59.2	4 12.1 36.4	33 55.0
Above 31	3 100 6.1		3 5.0
Total	*49* *81.7*	*11* *18.3*	*60* *100*

Chi-square = 3.40530	Min. E.F. = .550
D.F. = 2	Cells with E.F.<5 = 3 of 6 (50.0%)
Significance = .1822	No. of Missing observations = 0

Unless self-reliance is brought about, the impact will be less on literacy or on attitude towards the girl-child. Therefore the experiment tried to create self-reliance among the women of the village. Self-confidence or self-reliance is the main factor for the individual development. Education can create self-reliance to a large extent so that the development of the personality can be in a proper form. Unfortunately in the Indian society self-confidence or self-reliance is not emphasized either individually or collectively. The caste system prevailing in the Indian society gives very little room for the development of self-reliance. This is particularly true with the lower caste and those who live in the rural societies. Women by nature and by social circumstances are less confident and there is no mechanism to create confidence among them. As a result of this women lack confidence in themselves. The experiment conducted here showed initially that 45 per cent disagreed with the statement. "A women can look after a family". After the experiment 11.7 per cent neutral. This shows the impact of adult education which creates confidence in them.

Women always depend on somebody and this gives them a dependent personality. This is the main reason why women do not have the confidence in themselves. The social, economic or other activities are done

Table 6.9 : Attitude of the Women Towards the Statement "A Woman Can Look After A Family"

Before Experiment—Experimental Village

Respondents	*Agree*	*Neutral*	*Disagree*	*Total*
Below 20	9 37.5 36.0	2 8.3 25.0	13 54.2 40.1	24 40.0
21 to 30	15 45.5 60.0	5 15.2 62.5	13 39.4 48.1	33 55.0
Above 31	1 33.3 4.0	1 33.3 12.5	1 33.3 3.7	3 5.0
Total	*25* *41.7*	*8* *13.3*	*27* *45.0*	*60* *100*

Chi-square = 2.46481 Min. E.F. = .400
D.F. = 4 Cells with E.F.<5 = 5 of 9 (55.6%)
Significance = .6509 No. of Missing observations = 0

Table 6.9 A : Attitude of the Women Towards the Statement "A Woman Can Look After a Family"

After Experiment—Experimental Village

Respondents	*Agree*	*Disagree*	*Total*
Below 20	19 79.2 35.8	5 20.0 71.4	24 40.0
21 to 30	31 93.9 58.5	2 6.1 28.6	33 55.0
Above 31	3 100 5.7		3 5.0
Total	*53* *88.3*	*7* *11.7*	*60* *100*

Chi-square = 3.35947 Min. E.F. = .350
D.F. = 2 Cells with E.F.<5 = 4 of 6 (66.7%)
Significance = .1864 No. of Missing observations = 0

only with the support of men. 50 per cent of the women taken for this study believed that they could run the family only with male support (Table 6.10).

Table 6.10 : Attitude of the Women Towards the Statement "A Woman Can Look After the Family only with Male Support"

Before Experiment—Experimental Village

Respondents	*Agree*	*Neutral*	*Disagree*	*Total*
	7	2	15	24
Below 20	29.2	8.3	62.5	40.0
	23.3	50.0	57.7	
	22	2	9	33
21 to 30	66.7	6.1	27.3	55.0
	73.3	50.0	34.6	
	1		2	3
Above 31	33.3		66.7	5.0
	3.3		7.7	
	30	*4*	*26*	*60*
Total	*50.0*	*6.7*	*43.3*	*100*

Chi-square	= 8.77739	Min. E.F.	= .200
D.F.	= 4	Cells with E.F.<5 =	5 of 9 (55.6%)
Significance	= .0669	No. of Missing observations = 0	

Table 6.10 A : Attitude of the Women Towards the Statement "A Woman Can Look After the Family only with Male Support"

After Experiment—Experimental Village

Respondents	*Agree*	*Neutral*	*Disagree*	*Total*
	3	3	18	24
Below 20	12.5	12.5	75.0	40.0
	33.3	60.0	40.0	
	6	2	24	33
21 to 30	18.2	6.1	72.1	55.0
	66.7	40.0	53.3	
			3	3
Above 31			100	5.0
			6.7	
	10	*5*	*45*	*60*
Total	*16.7*	*8.3*	*75.0*	*100*

Chi-square	= 2.81818	Min. E.F.	= .050
D.F.	= 6	Cells with E.F.<5 =	10 of 12 (83.3%)
Significance	= .8313	No. of Missing observations = 0	

This attitude was changed after the experiment and it is shown here that only 15 per cent of the women respondents felt the need of the male support for running the family. In the rural societies women are considered a weaker section who cannot do any independent work, and therefore women think that they are physiologically weak to do the work of the house and income-generating jobs simultaneously. Atleast half of the respondents in the pre and post-study preserve this view. The adult education had no impact here. Even after the experiment 48.3 per cent of the women said that women could not do both the jobs simultaneously.

From this one can infer that adult education in some aspects had only very little impact on the rural folk. The deep-rooted ideas and values cannot be changed by a short term course. Girls are considered a burden to the family and thus they are kept inside the house, denying them education or employment. The social factors existing in the society do not permit the girls to take up education or employment. Women strongly believe that there is no need for girls to take up employment. Thus the study shows that respondents disagreed with the idea of giving an orientation for the girls to take up employment.

In fact, after the experiment, 43.3 per cent had this attitude, so here again the adult education was having less impact. The employment factor is negatively approached by the women respondents.

In the pre-study only 43.3 per cent had given this answer whereas in the post-study, 75 per cent said that they could do only supportive jobs.

This may be due to the fact that women were afraid that there were on jobs. This fear might have created a negative tendency towards employment. So the part-time work or supportive job, was in favour as they could give attention both to the family and to the job. Moreover society believes that women should not go out for work, because it is below the dignity and pride of the family for women to take up any job outside the family. Usually the men do not like women taking up jobs. In this study also 40 per cent of the women respondents before the experiment said that their men did not like them going for work. The same group of women later changed the attitude and only 18.3 per cent said that men would not like them to go for jobs.

However one should understand that society considers it a loss of prestige if women were to go for jobs. Perhaps the same society would allow girls to get educated but not allow them to take up employment. Thus 48.3 per cent of the women in the pre-study gave an answer that girls need not be given an orientation towards employment. If the girls have to be given orientation for jobs the same should be introduced in the schools. Government and voluntary agencies should come forward to give training to girls. A few respondents say that job-oriented courses should be introduced for girls but there is a larger section of women who say that job oriented courses should be introduced in schools for girls.

The impact of adult education can be seen in changing the attitude of women towards literacy and the girl-child but adult education did not have any impact in creating self-confidence. As a result of this there was no complete change in the attitude of women respondents. We can infer from this study a change in the attitude is possible only after a long duration of the course. A short-term course like this can change the attitude only to a certain extent. The result in the attitude towards women was negative before the experiment, but after the experiment there was an ambivalent situation for women towards themselves. They are neither definitely positive nor negative and a complete change is yet to be seen among them.

As the attitude is not completely changed, the women in the pre-study had a negative attitude towards the girls when asked about the equality of treatment for boys and girls in the family. Table 6.11 shows that 36.7% of the women respondents in the pre-study said that girls and boys should not be treated equally. This attitude changed later and most of the women said that they should be treated equally.

However 73.3 per cent (31) of the women in the pre-study (Table 6.12) and 86.7 per cent in the post-study (Table 6.12A) say that the girl children have to be given extra protection in the family. This is exactly an ambivalent situation prevailing in the minds of the women.

From the answers given by the women they still believe that girls are a different category who need special attention inside and outside the house. During infancy, adolescence and adulthood a girl is given extra protection, both physically and psychologically. The girl needs more attention than boys. 65 per cent of the women respondents in the pre-study (Table 6.13) and 90 per cent of the women respondents in the post-study (Table 6.13A) feel that girls should be given more support during adolescence than boys. The reason for this is that girls need more self-control than boys. The

Table 6.11 : Attitude of the Women Towards the Statement "Girl Children are to be Given Equal Treatment Alongwith the Boys in the Family"

Before Experiment—Experimental Village

Respondents	*Agree*	*Neutral*	*Disagree*	*Total*
	12	4	8	24
Below 20	50.0	16.7	33.3	40.0
	38.7	57.1	36.4	
	18	2	13	33
21 to 30	54.5	6.1	39.4	55.0
	58.1	28.6	59.1	
	1	1	1	3
Abcve 31	33.3	33.3	33.3	5.0
	3.2	14.3	4.5	
	31	*7*	*22*	*60*
Total	*51.7*	*11.7*	*36.7*	*100*

Chi-square	= 3.02015	Min. E.F.	= .350
D.F.	= 4	Cells with E.F.<5=	5 of 9 (55.6%)
Significance	= .5545	No. of Missing observations = 0	

Table 6.12 : Attitude of the Women Towards the Statement "Girl Children Have to be Given Extra Care in the Family"

Before Experiment—Experimental Village

Respondents	*Agree*	*Neutral*	*Disagree*	*Total*
	16	3	5	24
Below 20	66.7	12.5	20.8	40.0
	36.4	60.0	45.5	
	26	2	5	33
21 to 30	78.8	6.1	15.2	55.0
	59.1	40.0	45.5	
	2		1	3
Above 31	66.7		33.3	5.0
	4.5		9.1	
	44	*5*	*11*	*60*
Total	*73.3*	*8.3*	*18.3*	*100*

Chi-square	= 1.88430	Min. E.F.	= .250
D.F.	= 4	Cells with E.F.<5=	6 of 9 (66.7%)
Significance	= .7570	No. of Missing observations = 0	

Table 6.12 A : Attitude of the Women Towards the Statement "Girl Children Have to be Given Extra Care in the Family"

After Experiment—Experimental Village

Respondents	*Agree*	*Neutral*	*Disagree*	*Total*
Below 20	20 83.3 38.5		4 16.7 66.7	24 40.0
21 to 30	29 87.9 55.8	2 6.1 100.0	2 6.1 33.3	33 55.0
Above 31	3 100.0 5.8			3 5.0
Total	*52* *86.7*	*2* *3.3*	*6* *10.0*	*60* *100*

Chi-square	= 1.88430	Min. E.F.	= .250
D.F.	= 4	Cells with E.F.<5 =	6 of 9 (66.7%)
Significance	= .7570	No. of Missing observations = 0	

Table 6.13 : Attitude of the Women Towards the Statement "Girl Children Should be Given Much Moral Support in the Beginning of their Adulthood"

Before Experiment—Experimental Village

Respondents	*Agree*	*Neutral*	*Disagree*	*Total*
Below 20	14 58.3 35.9	6 25.0 46.2	4 16.7 50.0	24 40.0
21 to 30	22 66.7 56.4	7 21.2 53.8	4 12.1 50.0	33 55.0
Above 31	3 100 7.7			3 5.0
total	*39* *65.0*	*13* *21.7*	*8* *13.3*	*60* *100*

Chi-square	= 2.15618	Min. E.F.	= .400
D.F.	= 4	Cells with E.F.<5 =	5 of 9 (55.6%)
Significance	= .7071	No. of Missing observations = 0	

Table 6.13 A : Attitude of the Women Towards the Statement "Girl Children Should be Given Much Moral Support in the Beginning of their Adulthood"

After Experiment—Experimental Village

Respondents	*Agree*	*Neutral*	*Disagree*	*Total*
	20	3	1	24
Below 20	83.3	12.5	4.2	40.0
	37.0	60.0	100	
	31	2		33
21 to 30	93.9	6.1		55.0
	57.4	40.0		
	3			3
Above 31	100			50.0
	5.6			
	54	*5*	*1*	*60*
Total	*90.0*	*8.3*	*1.7*	*100*

Chi-square	= 2.66330	Min. E.F.	= .050
D.F.	= 4	Cells with E.F.<5 =	7 of 9 (77.8%)
Significance	= .6157	No. of Missing observations =	0

problems of marriage, child birth etc., should be tackled by women and they need great confidence and strength. In the rural society girls are treated as commodities and usually they are the tools of insult. Most of the women respondents say that it is this public insult which create a loss of confidence in them. As these values are deep-rooted in the society many women even after the experiment, believed that female infanticide was a better solution for the problems of women.

36.7 per cent of the women in the post-study (Table 6.14) said that it was better to kill the child as soon as the child was born. Majority of the women feel that the economic problem cannot be solved merely by getting education.

Thus 53.3 per cent of the women respondents in the pre-study (Table 6.15) and 31.7 per cent in the post-study (Table 6.15 A) felt that infanticide was a solution for their economic problems. As we have seen in the control village the women in the experiment village also did not see the female infanticide to be against religion. Almost half of women respondents say that it was not against the religion or the laws of the society.

Table 6.14 : Attitude of the Women Towards the Statement "Better to Kill the Child as soon as it is Born Instead of Allowing it to Face Problems Throughout Life"

After Experiment—Experimental Village

Respondents	*Agree*	*Neutral*	*Disagree*	*Total*
Below 20	11 45.8 50.0		13 54.2 36.1	24 40.0
21 to 30	9 66.7 9.1	2 6.1 100	22 33.3 2.8	33 5.0
Above 31	2 66.7 9.1		1 33.3 2.8	3 5.0
Total	*22* *36.7*	*2* *3.3*	*36* *60.0*	*60* *100*

Chi-square	= 4.45305	Min. E.F.	= .100
D.F.	= 4	Cells with E.F.<5 =	5 of 9 (55.6%)
Significance	= .3482	No. of Missing observations = 0	

Table 6.15 : Attitude of the Women Towards the Statement "Doing Away with the Child is a Better Solution Than Facing the Economic Problems"

Before Experiment—Experimental Village

Respondents	*Agree*	*Neutral*	*Disagree*	*Total*
Below 20	11 45.8 34.5	1 4.2 25.0	12 50.0 50.0	24 40.0
21 to 30	20 60.6 62.5	3 9.1 75.0	10 30.3 41.7	33 55.0
Above 31	1 33.3 3.1		2 66.7 8.3	3 5.0
Total	*32* *53.3*	*4* *6.7*	*24* *40.0*	*60* *100*

Chi-square	= 3.43040	Min. E.F.	= .200
D.F.	= 4	Cells with E.F.<5 =	5 of 9 (55.6%)
Significance	= .4885	No. of Missing observations = 0	

Table 6.15 A : Attitude of the Women Towards the Statement "Doing Away with the Child is a Better Solution Than Facing the Economic Problems"

After Experiment—Experimental Village

Respondents	*Agree*	*Neutral*	*Disagree*	*Total*
	8	3	13	24
Below 20	33.3	12.5	54.2	40.0
	42.1	60.0	36.1	
	9	2	22	33
21 to 30	27.3	6.1	66.7	55.0
	47.4	40.0	61.1	
	2		1	3
Above 31	66.7		33.3	5.0
	10.5		2.8	
	19	*5*	*36*	*60*
Total	*31.7*	*8.3*	*60.0*	*100*

Chi-square	= 3.07343	Min. E.F.	= .250
D.F.	= 4	Cells with E.F.<5 =	5 of 9 (55.6%)
Significance	= .5456	No. of Missing observations = 0	

Table 6.16 : Attitude of the Women Towards the Statement "Female Infanticide is Against Religion"

Before Experiment—Experimental Village

Respondents	*Agree*	*Neutral*	*Disagree*	*Total*
	7		17	24
Below 20	29.2		70.8	40.0
	43.8		42.5	
	8	4	21	33
21 to 30	24.2	12.1	63.6	55.0
	50.0	100	52.5	
	1		2	3
Above 31	33.3		66.7	5.0
	6.3		5.0	
	16	*4*	*40*	*60*
Total	*26.7*	*6.7*	*66.7*	*100*

Chi-square	= 3.55966	Min. E.F.	= .200
D.F.	= 4	Cells with E.F.<5 =	5 of 9 (55.6%)
Significance	= .4689	No. of Missing observations = 0	

Table 6.16 A : Attitude of the Women Towards the Statement "Female Infanticide is Against Religion"

After Experiment—Experimental Village

Respondents	*Agree*	*Neutral*	*Disagree*	*Total*
Below 20	12 50.0 48.0	1 4.2 100	11 45.8 32.4	24 40.0
21 to 30	11 33.3 44.0		22 66.7 64.7	33 55.0
Above 31	2 66.7 8.0		1 33.3 2.9	3 5.0
Total	*25* *41.7*	*1* *1.7*	*34* *56.7*	*60* *100*

Chi-square	= 4.26765	Min. E.F.	= .050
D.F.	= 4	Cells with E.F.<5 =	5 of 9 (55.6%)
Significance	= .3710	No. of Missing observations = 0	

They say that the society permits to kill the child and therefore it is not against the laws of society.

Table 6.17 : Attitude of the Women Towards the Statement "Female Infanticide is Against the Law of the Society"

Before Experiment—Experimental Village

Respondents	*Agree*	*Neutral*	*Disagree*	*Total*
Below 20	3 12.5 37.5	2 8.3 28.6	19 79.2 42.2	24 40.0
21 to 30	4 12.1 50.0	5 15.2 71.4	24 72.7 53.3	33 55.0
Above 31	1 33.3 12.5		2 66.7 4.4	3 5.0
Total	*8* *13.3*	*7* *11.7*	*45* *75.0*	*60* *100*

Chi-square	= 1.97700	Min. E.F.	= .350
D.F.	= 4	Cells with E.F.<5 =	7 of 9 (77.8 %)
Significance	= .7400	No. of Missing observations = 0	

Table 6.17 A : Attitude of the Women Towards the Statement "Female Infanticide is Against the Law of the Society"

After Experiment—Experimental Village

Respondents	*Agree*	*Disagree*	*Total*
	18	6	24
Below 20	75.0	25.0	40.0
	54.5	22.2	
	13	20	33
21 to 30	39.4	60.6	55.0
	39.4	74.1	
	2	1	3
Above 31	66.7	33.3	5.0
	6.1	3.7	
Total	*33*	*27*	*60*
	55.0	*45.0*	*100*

Chi-square	= 7.29109	Min. E.F.	= 1.350
D.F.	= 2	Cells with E.F.<5 =	2 of 6 (33.3 %)
Significance	= .0261	No. of Missing Observations = 0	

However most of the women respondents after the experiment regretted and said that God might punish them for killing the children (Table 6.18 A).

The study clearly presents the attitude of women towards female infanticide. Women like girls but they are not in favour of bringing them up because the rules of the society do not permit them to bring the child up in their own way and hence they are forced to kill the child. The study showed that female infanticide cannot totally be eliminated merely by adult education. Adult education has made the women respondents think about the phenomenon from many angles.

The introduction of adult education in Nadumuthalaikulam was the external stimulus given to the people as part of the experiment. The experiment was carried out to find the impact of adult education on female infanticide taking into consideration the elements of change, the attitude towards literacy, attitude towards the girl-child, attitude towards self-reliance and attitude towards female infanticide. The experiment showed that a considerable difference of opinion existed between the opinions of the control and experiment villages.

Table 6.18 : Attitude of the Women Towards the Statement "Those Who Kill the Female Children will be Punished by God"

Before Experiment—Experimental Village

Respondents	*Agree*	*Neutral*	*Disagree*	*Total*
Below 20		4 16.7 50.0	20 83.3 43.5	24 40.0
21 to 30	5 15.2 83.3	4 12.1 50.0	24 72.7 52.2	33 55.0
Above 31	1 33.3 16.7		2 66.7 4.3	3 5.0
Total	*6* *10.0*	*8* *13.3*	*46* *76.7*	*60* *100*

Chi-square	= 5.79051	Min. E.F.	= .300
D.F.	= 4	Cells with E.F.<5 =	7 of 9 (77.8 %)
Significance	= .2153	No. of Missing observations = 0	

Table 6.18 A : Attitude of the Women Towards the Statement "Those Who Kill the Female Children will be Punished by God"

After Experiment—Experimental Village

Respondents	*Agree*	*Neutral*	*Disagree*	*Total*
Below 20	22 91.7 43.1	1 4.2 33.3	1 4.2 16.7	24 40.0
21 to 30	26 78.8 51.0	2 6.1 66.7	5 15.2 83.3	33 55.0
Above 31	3 100 5.9			3 5.0
Total	*51* *85.0*	*3* *5.0*	*6* *10.0*	*60* *100*

Chi-square	= 2.60472	Min. E.F.	= .150
D.F.	= 4	Cells with E.F.<5 =	7 of 9 (77.8 %)
Significance	= .6260	No. of Missing observations = 0	

Adult education impressed upon the people of the experimental village, the need for educating themselves in inculcating self-reliance and the change of attitude towards the girl-child. Thus the importance of adult education was clearly brought out by the experiment.

7

Conclusion

The present study which analyses the female infanticide in two selected villages viz., Kupanampatti and Nadumuthalaikulam, suggests that adult education programmes could be useful in the long run in eliminating this problem. Female infanticide is a contemporary problem for the social scientists especially of Women Studies, but it is an age-old problem for the historians too. The social scientists, the administrators, the feminists and the planners view female infanticide as a woman's problem as this phenomenon contributes to the lowering of the woman's status. Therefore the society considers female infanticide to be an indicator of the backwardness of women.

The status of woman was not uniform either region-wise or period-wise. During the Vedic period the position of woman was not inferior, as she had a respectable position during that time. The Epic period also assigned a definite role to woman which required mental strength and stamina, not inferior to that of man. In later Hindu literature the position of woman varied and many works recognised the authority of patriarchy. As a result, women were depicted simultaneously as fertile and benevolent or aggressive and destructive. Many, the Law-Giver of Hinduism has assigned a dependent status to women which is considered a major principle of Hinduism. According to Manu, a woman should be dependent throughout her life and this belief continued to exist in the Hindu society.

When women were assigned a low position in society they started facing many problems. Society treated women on par with domestic animals and they were not given property rights or rights over other possessions. Thus women were considered a burden to the society. The society's development has not solved the problems of women. On the contrary it has only increased the problems. For all the evils in the society women were blamed and women themselves had a low opinion of themselves. This psychological state of mind has resulted in killing the female child by the women as an escape from problems.

The problem of female infanticide is both historical phenomenon and a contemporary phenomenon. History reveals that several parts of the world at different times, had indulged in infanticide as a result of custom or superstition. Today female infanticide in more a sociological problem than a religious problem. The legal sanction prohibit the phenomenon, but socially it is accepted by certain societies. Thus one can say that a phenomenon becomes a social process if there is social approval. Female infanticide is one such phenomenon.

In modern society, female infanticide is practised by certain sections of the society because of the extreme problems faced by the women. In India female infanticide is seen in Tamil Nadu, Rajasthan and in some other parts of the country. The present investigation concentrates on Tamil Nadu, as female infanticide largely prevails in certain parts of the state, especially in the districts of Madurai. Therefore the study was conducted in the district of Madurai where the female infanticide is still being practised. After a pilot study it was found that Usilampatti taluk had the maximum number of female infanticide cases and therefore two villages were selected for the study from this area with the following objectives.

1) To study the pattern of female infanticide in two select villages.

In order to reduce female infanticide a change in attitude is necessary and therefore the second objective aims at—

2) Changing the attitude of women towards women with special reference to female infanticide.

This study tries to change the attitude through an external stimulus, namely education. Hence the next objective is—

3) To study the impact of adult education on the rate of female infanticide.

Changing the attitude is not the end. The main goal of this study is to suggest steps for eliminating female infanticide. In order to achieve this, one should know the various ways and means to reduce the rate of female infanticide.

In order to achieve the objective mentioned above the following other objectives have also to be met.

4) Evolving an adult education kit which can be used in those areas where the female infanticide is practised.
5) Evolving other education tools like video films, adult education primer and audio cassettes.

The district of Madurai was taken as the universe, though Usilampatti taluk was the main area of the study. In Usilampatti taluk two villages were selected for detailed analysis and for the experiment of adult education. One village namely Kuppanampatti was kept as a control village and another namely Nadumuthalaikulam was the experimental village. The two villages were selected in such a way that the influence of one village did not affect the other village. The experimental design used in this study was found to be effective as there was no external influence during the period when the experiment was conducted. There was also no natural calamities affecting the village. The unit of the study was the household, for understanding female infanticide, and females were considered for attitudinal study. The data were collected in the experimental village and the control village through an interviewed schedule and through interviews. Tape recorder, video cassettes, audio cassettes, learning kits etc., were used for adult education programmes. Age, education occupation, income and marital status were used as variables for the analyses of the data.

The results of the study show that female infanticide is a symptom of underdevelopment and decay of the society. Therefore the problem is to be considered seriously. The practice of female infanticide is approached through two angles. In this study, the first approach is a traditional one where the women kill female children out of fear and the second a modern one where the female infanticide results in economic savings for the society. In both the cases the victims are females. The female infanticide is defined as a practice of killing a female baby immediately after birth by resorting to such practices and techniques like deliberate delay in feeding, non-feeding or less feeding.

General causes of female infanticide are either economic issues or social issues. The economic causes include poverty, and unemployment and social causes include customs, ceremony, ritual etc. Thus one can conclude that it is the social and economic conditions which force the women to kill their babies.

Female infanticide affects the immediate society as well as the larger society. When the mother, the father and the siblings and affected by killing the child in the family, the larger community feels ashamed. Female infanticide results in psychological shocks. Therefore they keep the fact as a secret though the practice is very common in the community.

The case studies in the present study reveal that the main motivating factors behind the killings are poverty, social discrimination and religious feelings. It is found that the motivators generally are the husbands and relatives.

In India the caste stratification has given different statuses to people and women are no exception to this. Women in lover castes face all problems which make life difficult. Their problems vary from region to region and Tamil Nadu has a complicated network of castes, and it experiences the related consequences. The caste values and norms are more numerous in rural areas than in cities and towns. It is a custom to practise all rituals and ceremonies of the caste, the neglect of which will lead to the ostracization of the members of the community. The poverty in rural areas of Tamil Nadu which results from bad agricultural seasons, intensifies the problems of the rural people who are strictly under the control of the caste system. Poverty, combined with the rigid rules of the caste, is the main cause of female infanticide in the community selected. The Kallars have very low status in the caste hierarchy. Traditionally they have an occupation of guarding other communities though today they are designated as a denotified community.

The study found that the women of this community were extraordinarily brave during ancient days, and they used to take care of the family in the absence of their men. Kallar women who were settled in rural areas of Usilampatti were not able to recognize their status in the changing society. They were not familiar with the concept of status, of economic freedom or of social justice. Thus the women of Usilampatti area continue to live in the traditional way. In both the villages selected, it was found that the women were mostly illiterate. The study decided to proceed to change the attitude of women towards, themselves against their socio-economic background. One can find that a major solution for female infanticide is an attitudinal change. In an area like this the attitudinal change is possible only through an external stimulus. The socio-economic background of the area shows that most of the women are illiterate, without proper occupation or an independent income. It was decide to try an experiment of an external stimulus on one of the villages. The external stimulus was an adult education programme which was given in Nadumuthalaikulam village for a period of three months. In both the villages, sixty females were selected from sixty households for the experiments whose age ranged from 15-35 years. The women of this group selected because it is these people who are the mothers and socializing agents for the female children.

Adult education programmes for this group were designed taking care of their background. An adult education kit was prepared including visual programmes and programmes like songs, stories, dialogues, skits etc. This was effective because most of them were interested in cinema and in listening to stories or viewing plays. The Indian rural areas where women are backward, the attitudinal change has to be brought about not only through literacy programmes but also through others means of education. Before adult education was introduced, the attitudes of the women towards themselves and towards female infanticide were measured using an attitudinal scale. Forty items were prepared on a three-point scale and suitable weightage was given for measuring the attitude. The attitude scale was administered in both the village before the experiment started, and again after the completion of the experiment. The attitude of women were measured in Nadumuthalaikulam and Kuppanampatti. The experiment was the introduction of the adult education programme in one of the villages namely Nadumuthalaikulam where the households were categorised into two groups consisting of thirty families each.

In the control village the women were not exposed to adult education, and the attitude was measured after an interval of three months. The results show that the basic attitude of women did not change in Kuppanampatti towards literacy, the girl child, self-reliance and female infanticide.

In Kupanampatti village the concept of education was absent and this state continued even after an interval of another three months. Women's education was not considered essential by the women of Kuppanampatti village. The women of Kupanampatti village did not agree with the idea that school education would help in developing society. They felt that if the economic background was sound, education was not necessary either for women or for men. However 28.3 per cent of the women felt that they would become literate if they were given an opportunity. Though this was a minority, it was significant that atleast a few women were taking the concept of education seriously. These women could become models for the society and could be guided properly to lead the rest of the society. The control village showed a negative attitude towards literacy. Attitude towards the girl-child was also negative in this village, both in the pre-study as well as in the post-study. Kuppanampati women felt that female children were burden to the family and the society. As the female child meant expenses they considered the male child as an asset. Religion also supports the view that the male child is essential for a family. The village sanctions and social values developed a negative attitude towards the girl-child in the control village.

Women were not self-confident. The study says that the women of Kuppanampatti did not consider themselves independent and therefore they considered male support essential. In the control village the females said that women could not do the house-hold jobs and income-generating jobs simultaneously. Also they considered that jobs were not necessary for women. Therefore they felt that the girls need not be given job-oriented courses either.

As the negative tendency of women increases, the tendency towards female infanticide also increases. When there is a negative attitude towards literacy, the girl child and self-reliance it is but natural to have the tendency towards female infanticide. Here it was found that when the natural tendency of the growth was hampered, the society resorted to other ways to escape from the problems.

This is evident in the experimental village. The three-months adult education programme considerably changed the attitude of women towards literacy, towards the girl-child, towards self-reliance and therefore towards female infanticide. In the experimental village the results showed that the adult education had considerably changed the outlook of the females. The Adult education which emphasized the importance of education gave the women respondents an idea that education could help a person in different ways. The women respondents said that after the experiment education would help in every-day life and therefore they considered it necessary for women. They also came out with the idea that progress could be achieved, through school education and therefore education was necessary for both boys and girls. The adult education kit emphasized the importance of education in leading happy married life. This also influenced the women as they became aware of the fact that education could improve marital life by giving competence and courage to meet calamities and problems.

After three months of implementing adult education programmes in the experimental village, women changed their attitude towards the girl-child. The change in the attitude in this regard was slow. Here women respondents were in a dilemma though the results showed a marginal change. They firmly believed that girls were a burden to the family but the number of women who stuck to this idea was less after the experiment. One should not at this point that the attitude towards the girl child would change only if the society changed. As long as the society and the present values existed in the society attitude towards the girl-child and her problems would continue to exist. Thus the Kuppanampatti women did not change completely their attitude towards the girl child.

The adult education programmes had given them a self-confidence. This was proved through the experiment when women felt that they could look after the family by themselves, if an emergency occurred. The influence of adult education programmes created a new awareness towards employment. They felt that women could do income-generating jobs and therefore the girls should be given suitable orientation towards jobs from the childhood itself.

However one cannot say that attitude of the women had completely changed. They feel the girls should be given extra-protection in the family as they are a special category during infancy, adolescence and during adulthood. As long as the values of the society remain the same, the problems of women also will remain the same. This was the feeling of most of the women in the experimental village after the experiment. However they said that female infanticide was a way for the women to escape from the problems of the society. The adult education programme had given them a new awareness and made them realise that female infanticide was an evil and a sinful act.

To conclude one can say that education has given a new awareness to the women who were once ignorant. The study shows that ignorance is the real cause of female infanticide which can be removed through education. Thus indirectly education can be said to be the proper solution for female infanticide.

$$\text{Before Experiment Ignorance} \xrightarrow{\hspace{3em}} +\text{F I}$$

$$\text{After Experiment Ignorance} \xrightarrow[\text{Adult Education}]{\text{Experiment}} -\text{F I}$$

The solution for female infanticide is to be seen in the society itself. Education should be provided to the women and employment should be generated to eradicate poverty which in turn would given better status to the women. The social evils existing in the society can also be removed through education. Thus adult education should be considered a means and a first step in bringing about awareness to women which would provide a solution for female infanticide.

Appendices

APPENDIX—I

Attitude of Women Towards Literacy

CONTROL VILLAGE I — KUPPANAMPATTI

Statistics from TWOMV

First Sample Mean	7.1000
Second Sample Mean	6.9000
First Sample Variance	7.6103
Second Sample Variance	2.5759
First Sample Valid Observations	30.0000
Second Sample Valid Observations	30.0000
First Sample Missing Values	0.0000
Second Sample Missing Values	0.0000

Mean Inferences Assuming Equal Variances

Pooled Variance	5.0931
T Value	.3432
Probability of a Larger T in ABS. Value	.7327
Degrees of Freedom	58.0000

Mean Inferences Assuming Unequal Variances

T Value	.3432
Approx. Prob. of a Larger T in ABS. Value	.7330
Degrees of Freedom	46.6134

Variance Inferences

F Value	2.95448
Probability of a Larger F in ABS. Value	.00471
Degrees of Freedom	2.95448

BO = 6.41 B1 = .06932

Stat

Mean of X	Mean of Y	Variance of Y	Variance of Y	Corr.	Std. Err. Bo
7.1	6.9	7.61	2.576	.1192	.8297

Std. Err. B1	Df Reg.	SS Reg.	DF Error	SS Error	PTS NAN
0.1092	1	1.061	22	73.64	0

Univariate Statistics from UVSTA

	1	2
Mean	7.10	6.90
Variance	7.61	2.58
Std. Dev.	2.76	1.60
Skewness	1.47	.42
Kurtosis	2.82	.90
Minimum	3.00	4.00
Maximum	16.00	11.00
Range	13.00	7.00
Coef. Var.	.39	.23
Count	30.00	30.00
Lower Clm	6.07	6.30
Upper Clm	8.13	7.50
Lowr Clv	4.83	1.63
Upper Clv	13.75	4.66

APPENDIX—II

Attitude of Women Towards Literacy

CONTROL VILLAGE II — KUPPANAMPATTI

Statistics from TWOMV

First Sample Mean	7.3667
Second Sample Mean	6.0333
First Sample Variance	8.0333
Second Sample Variance	2.7230
First Sample Valid Observations	30.0000
Second Sample Valid Observations	30.0000
First Sample Missing Values	0.0000
Second Sample Missing Values	0.0000

Mean Inferences Assuming Equal Variances

Pooled Variance	5.3782
T Value	2.2267
Probability of a Larger T in ABS. Value	.0299
Degrees of Freedom	58.0000

Mean Inferences Assuming Unequal Variances

T Value	2.2267
Approx. Prob. of a Larger T in ABS. Value	.0308
Degrees of Freedom	46.6337

Variance Inferences

F Value	2.95019
Probability of a Larger F in ABS. Value	.00477
Degrees of Freedom	2.95019

BO = 5.48 B1 = .07569

Stat

Mean of X	Mean of Y	Variance of Y	Variance of Y	Corr.	Std. Err. Bo
7.367	6.033	8.033	2.723	.13	.8592

Std. Err. B1	Df Reg.	SS Reg.	DF Error	SS Error	PTS NAN
0.1091	1	1.335	28	77.63	0

Univariate Statistics from UVSTA

	1	2
Mean	7.37	6.03
Variance	8.03	2.72
Std. Dev.	2.83	1.65
Skewness	.91	1.12
Kurtosis	.13	.23
Minimum	4.00	4.00
Maximum	15.00	10.00
Range	11.00	6.00
Coef. Var.	.38	.27
Count	30.00	30.00
Lower Clm	6.31	5.42
Upper Clm	8.43	6.65
Lowr Clv	5.10	1.73
Upper Clv	14.52	4.92

APPENDIX—II

Attitude of Women Towards Literacy

EXPERIMENTAL VILLAGE II — NADUMUTHALAIKULAM

Statistics from TWOMV

First Sample Mean	4.9667
Second Sample Mean	19.9000
First Sample Variance	6.3782
Second Sample Variance	4.3000
First Sample Valid Observations	30.0000
Second Sample Valid Observations	30.0000
First Sample Missing Values	0.0000
Second Sample Missing Values	0.0000

Mean Inferences Assuming Equal Variances

Pooled Variance	5.3391
T Value	–25.0305
Probability of a Larger T in ABS. Value	0.0000
Degrees of Freedom	58.0000

Mean Inferences Assuming Unequal Variances

T Value	–25.0305
Approx. Prob. of a Larger T in ABS. Value	.0000
Degrees of Freedom	55.8834

Variance Inferences

F Value	1.48329
Probability of a Larger F in ABS. Value	.29412
Degrees of Freedom	1.48329

BO = 19.07 B1 = .16706

Stat

Mean of X	Mean of Y	Variance of Y	Variance of Y	Corr.	Std. Err. Bo
4.967	19.9	6.378	4.3	.2035	.8436

Std. Err. B1	Df Reg.	SS Reg.	DF Error	SS Error	PTS NAN
.1519	1	5.162	28	119.5	0

Univariate Statistics from UVSTA

	1	2
Mean	4.97	19.90
Variance	6.38	4.30
Std. Dev.	2.53	2.07
Skewness	.06	–3.73
Kurtosis	–.79	15.71
Minimum	0.00	10.00
Maximum	10.00	22.00
Range	10.00	12.00
Coef. Var.	.51	.10
Count	30.00	30.00
Lower Clm	4.02	19.13
Upper Clm	5.91	20.67
Lowr Clv	4.05	2.73
Upper Clv	11.53	7.77

APPENDIX—IV

Attitude of Women Towards Literacy

EXPERIMENTAL VILLAGE II — NADUMUTHALAIKULAM

Statistics from TWOMV

First Sample Mean	6.6667
Second Sample Mean	19.4000
First Sample Variance	7.8851
Second Sample Variance	1.4207
First Sample Valid Observations	30.0000
Second Sample Valid Observations	30.0000
First Sample Missing Values	0.0000
Second Sample Missing Values	0.0000

Mean Inferences Assuming Equal Variances

Pooled Variance	4.6529
T Value	–22.8627
Probability of a Larger T in ABS. Value	0.0000
Degrees of Freedom	58.0000

Mean Inferences Assuming Unequal Variances

T Value	–22.8627
Approx. Prob. of a Larger T in ABS. Value	.0000
Degrees of Freedom	39.1216

Variance Inferences

F Value	5.55016
Probability of a Larger F in ABS. Value	.00001
Degrees of Freedom	5.55016

BO = 19.23 B1 = .02624

Stat

Mean of X	Mean of Y	Variance of Y	Variance of Y	Corr.	Std. Err. Bo
6.667	19.4	7.885	1.421	.6182	.5777

Std. Err. B1	Df Reg.	SS Reg.	DF Error	SS Error	PTS NAN
.08006	1	.1574	28	41.04	0

Univariate Statistics from UVSTA

	1	2
Mean	6.67	19.40
Variance	7.89	1.42
Std. Dev.	2.81	1.19
Skewness	1.27	−1.81
Kurtosis	1.96	2.12
Minimum	3.00	16.00
Maximum	15.00	20.00
Range	12.00	4.00
Coef. Var.	.42	.06
Count	30.00	30.00
Lower Clm	5.62	18.95
Upper Clm	7.72	19.85
Lowr Clv	5.00	.90
Upper Clv	14.25	2.57

Bibliography

Amit Kumar Gupta. *Women and Society: The Governmental Perspective.* New Delhi: Criterion Publication, 1986.

Aness Jung. *Unveiling India: A Woman 's Journey.* New Delhi: Penguin Books Private Ltd., 1987.

Antony, M.J. *Women's Rights: Everything an Indian Woman must know about her Rights in Plain Language.* New Delhi: Dialogue Publications, 1985.

Ashok Mitra. Adhiv Srimany and Lalit P. Pathak. *The State of Women: Household and Non-Household Ecnomic Activity.* New Delhi: Allied Publishers Pvt. Ltd., 1979.

Augustine, S. John (Ed.). *The Indian Family in Transition.* Bangalore: Christian Institute for the Stury of Religion and Society, 1982.

Baker, Mary and Anne. *Women To-day: A Multidisciplinary Approach to Women's Studies.* California: Brooks Cole Publishing Company, 1980.

Balse, Maya. *The Indian Female Attitude Towards Sex.* New Delhi: Chetana Publication, 1982.

Barret, Michele. *Women's Oppression To-day.* London: Villers Publication Ltd., 1980.

Bewles, Gloria and Klein Perate Duelli, *Theories of Women's Studies*. London: Routledge and Kegan Paul, 1983.

Bhatia, K.K., K.S. Kadhan, P.C. Chadala and S. Sharma. *A Treatise on the Current Problems in Indian Education*. New Delhi: Prakash Brothers. 1981.

Bhatia, S. C. and Srivastava. *Literacy. Literacy Materials and their Preparation: A General Perspective*. New Delhi: Directorate of Adult Education, 1978.

Bhoite, Anuradha. *Women Employees and Rural Development*. Delhi: Gian publishing House, 1987.

Bordia, Anil. *Adult Education in India*. New Delhi: Adult Education Association, 1973.

Bose, K. *Forward Block: A Sociological Profile of Mukkulathor's*. Madras: Tamil Nadu Academy of Political Science, 1988.

Bourchier, David. *The Feminist Challenge*. London: Macmillan Press, 1983.

Chanvet, John. *Modern Ideologies: Feminism*. London: J. M. Dent and Sons Ltd., 1982.

Clennon Lynda. M. *Women and Dualism*. New York: Longman Inc., 1979.

Crindle, J. W. M. (Tr.), *Megastheness Fragments*. XXVII.

Desai Neera. *Women in Modern India*. Bombay: Vora and Co. Publishers Pvt. Ltd., 1987.

Desai Neera and Maithreye Krishnaraj, *Women and Society in India*. Ajantha Publication, 1987.

Desai Neera and Vibhuti Patel. *Indian women: Change and Challenge in the International Decade 1975-85*. Bombay: Popular Prakashan, 1985.

Diwan, Paras. *Dowry and Protection to Married Women*. New Delhi: Deep and Deep Publications, 1987.

Everest, Janna Matson. *Women and Social Change in India*. New Delhi: Heritage Publishers, 1981.

Feinstein Karen, W. (e d.), *Working Women and Families*. London: Sage Publications, 1979.

Gulati Leela. *Profile in Female Poverty*. Delhi: Hindustan Publishing House, 1984.

Gupta, B.V. *Revolutions and Status of Women in India*: New Delhi: 1982.

Indira J. Parikh and Garg Pulink. *Indian Women: An Inner Dialogue*. New Delhi: Sage Publication, 1989.

Jacobson Dor Anne and Sasans Wadley. *Women in India: Two Perspectives*. New Delhi: Manohar Publications, 1986.

Jain, S. C. *Women and Technology*. Jaipur: Rawat Publications, 1985.

Jana Matson Evereti. *Women and Social Change in India*. Heritage Publication, 1985.

Jayagopal, R. (ed.), *Students in Extension Activities*. New Delhi: Indian University Association of Continuing Education, 1984.

Jessei B. Tellies, Nayak and Selena Casta Pinto. *Towards Self-Reliance: Income Generation for Women*. New Delhi: Satprakashan Sanchar Kendra, Satprachar Press Publication, June 1982.

Kapur, Promilla. *Marriage and the Working Women in India*. New Delhi: Vikas Publishing House, 1970.

Kothari, C.R. *Research Methodology, Methods and Techniques*. New Delhi: Wiley Eastern limited, 1985.

Kundu, C.L. *Adult Education: Principles, Practice and Prospects*. New Delhi: Sterling Publishers, 1986.

Lebra, Joyce. *Women and Work in India: Continuity*. New Delhi: Promilla and Company, 1984.

Leelamma Devasia and V. V. Devasial *Girl Child in India*. New Delhi: Ashish Publishing House, 1991.

Madan C. Paul, *Dowry and Prostitution in Women in India: A Study of Delhi Metropolis*. New Delhi: Swa India Publications, 1985, p. 7.

Maithreyi Krishna Raj. *Women Studies in India: Some Perspectives*. New Delhi: Sangam Books Publishers, 1986, p. 87.

Maithreyi Krishna Raj. *Women and Development*. Bombay: SNDT Women University, 1988, p. 132.

Manohar, Murali (ed.). *Socio-Economic Status of Indian Women*. Delhi: Seema Publications, 1983.

Mastry Chen, Manish Mitra, Geetha Athreya, Ahila Dholakia, Preetha Lal and Aruna Rao. *Indian Women*. New Delhi: Vikas Publishing House Pvt. Ltd., 1986.

Mazumdar, Vina. *Role of Rural Women in Development*. Bombay. Allied Publishers, 1978.

Mazumdar, Vina (ed.). *Women and Rural Transformation*. New Delhi: Concept Publishing Company, 1983.

Paul, M. C. *Dowry and Prostitution of Women in India: A Study of Delhi Metropolis*. New Delhi: Swa Indian Publications, 1985.

Peggas, J. *Cries of Agony: An Historical Account of Suttee, Infanticide, Ghat Murder and Slavery in India*. New Delhi: Discovery Publishing House, 1979.

Prem Lath Sharma. *Rural Women in Education*. New Delhi: Sterling Publishers Pvt. Ltd., 1988.

Ragozin A. Zanaide. *Vedic India*.

Ramnath Sharma. *Principles of Sociology*. New Delhi: Media Promoters and Publishers Pvt. Ltd., 1969.

Rani, Kala. *Role Conflict in Working Women*. New Delhi: Chetana Publications, 1976.

Rao, M.S.A. (ed.), *Social Movement in India*. New Delhi: Manohar Publications, 1979.

Rao, Usha. *Women in a Developing Society*. Delhi: Ashish Publishing House, 1983.

Reddy, Rehunanda. *Changing Status of Educational Working Women*. Delhi: B.R. Publishing Corporation, 1986.

Rekha Mehra, K. Saradamani. *Women and Rural Information*. New Delhi: Concept Publishing Company, 1983.

Saravanavel, P. *ResearchMethodology*. New Delhi: Kitab Mahal Publishers, 1987.

Sebasti, L. Raj S. J. *Quest for Gender Justice: A Critique of the Status of Women in India*. New Delhi: T.R. Publications for Satya Nilayam, 1991.

Shah, Kalpana. *Women's Liberation and Voluntary Action*. Delhi: Ajantha Publications, 1984.

Sharan, Raka. *Indian Women Workers*. Delhi: Cosmos Publications, 1985.

Sharma, Sita Ram. *Development of Adult Education in India*. New Delhi: Akasdeep Publishing House, First Edn. 1990.

Sharma Tripat. *Women in Ancient India: From A.D. 300 to 1200*. New Delhi: Ess Ess Publication, 1982.

Srivastave, Vinita. *Employment of Educated Married Women in India*. New Delhi: National Publishing House, 1978.

Stanley Liz and Wise Swe. *Breaking Out: Feminist Consciousness and Feminist Research*. London: Routlet and Kegan Paul, 1983.

Suchitra Anant, S.V. Ramani Rao and Kabitra Kapoor. *Women at Work in India*. New Delhi: (Institute of Social Studies Trust Sponsored by Ministry of Labour, Government of India) Sage Publications, 1986.

Susila Mehta. *Revolution and Status of Women in India*. New Delhi : Metropolitan Books (P) Ltd., 1982.

Tara Ali Baig. *Women of India*. New Delhi: Publications Division, Ministry of Information and Broadcasting, Government of India, May 1990.

Wallace A. Ruth. *Contemporary Sociological Theory*. Eagle Wood Cliffs: Alision Wolf, N. J., 1980.

Women Education, Equality: A Decade of Experiment. Paris: The UNESCO Press, 1975.

Journals

Barse, Sheela, "Rights of the Girl Child", *Indian Journal of Social Work*. 51 (1) January 1991.

Bhogle, Shalini, "Child Rearing Practices and Behaviour Development of a Girl Child" *Indian Journal of Social Welfare*, 52(1) January, 1991.

Bordia Anil. "Adult Education in India", *Indian Journal of Adult Education*. New Delhi, 1973.

Dutta S. C. "From Literacy to Liberation", *Indian Journal of Adult Education*, Vol. I (Dr. Zakir Hussain Memorial Lectures from 1970-1985), August 1986.

Gurusamy, S. and S. C. Kubendran, "A Decade for the Girls Child (1991-2000)", *Social Welfare*, Vol. xxxvii, No. 11-12, February - March 1991, p. 16.

"Penn Kulanthaigal Piranthathum Kolai", *Junior Viketan* (T), November 1990, pp. 4-5.

Ragavan, G. N. "Communication in India: Prospects and Policty", *Indian Journal of Adult Education*, Vol. XLV, N. 728, July-August 1984.

Seth, M., R.N. Mehrotra and B. Roy. "Attitude of Women Towards Literacy: Delhi Experiment", *Indian Journal of Adult Education*, Vol. XLIV, No, 5, May 1983, pp. 4-5.

Sharma. R.R. "Adult Education for Women", *Indian Journal of Adult Education*, Vol. XLIII, No. 2, February 2982, pp. 10-11.

Sheela C. Nuna. "Literacy Scenario in India during 1991: A March towards Development of Underdeveloped", Vol. XLI, No. 4, October - December 1991, p. 462.

Newspapers

"Child have Special Rights", *National Herald*, December 23, 1990.

"Documents on Education Proposes Basic Reforms", *Indian Express*, Madras, August 24, 1985.

"Drug Intake Increasing among Girls", *Times of India*, December 26, 1990.

"Ending Girl Infanticide", *Indian Express*, Madurai, May 28, 1990.

"Every Girl Child Needs Proper Care", *The Hindu*, December 19, 1990.

"Female Infanticide Still Persists", *Indian Express*, Madurai, October 29, 1990

"Focus on Saving the Girl Child", *The Hindu*, Madras, February 2, 1991.

"Government Steps to Prevent Female Infanticide", *Indian Express*, Madurai, November 12, 1990.

Gurusamy, S., "Female Infanticide: The Ugly Reality", *The Hindu*, November 11, 1990.

"Movement to Save Girl Child Urged". *The Hindustan Times*. December 23, 1990.

"Sex Determination or Extermination?" *The Hindu* (Weekly Magazine), Madurai, January 16, 1991).

"The Girl Child: A Social Victim", *The Times of India*, September 24, 1990.

"The Lesser Sex", *Indian Express*, Madurai, October 28, 1990.

"To be Born Girl is Curse", *The Hindustan Times*. December 12, 1990.

Reports

Adhiseshiah, Malcom S. *Adult Education and Inequality*. Madras: University of Madras, Report of the International Symposium (UNESCO), 1980.

Adult Education for Women in the Changing Pattern of Society, New Delhi: Report of the National Seminar. October 27-30, 1968.

Census of India, Primary Census Abstracts and Village and Town Directories of Madurai District. Tamil Nadu Census, 1971.

Census of India, Provisional Totals, Population and Literates by Residence and Sex of Madurai District, TAmil Nadu Census, 1991.

Annual Report 1983-84. New Delhi: Government of India, Ministry of Information and Broadcasting, 1984.

Challenge of Education: A Policy Perspective, New Delhi: Government of India, Ministry of Education, 1985.

National Literacy Mission, New Delhi: Government of India, Ministry of Human Resource Development, 1988.

International Literacy Year 1990": Action in India. New Delhi: Government of India, Ministry of Human Resource Development, Department of Education, 1990

Literacy Mission, Vol. XIL, N. 8, 1991.

"Literacy: A People's Movement", *National Literacy Mission*. New Delhi: Government of India, Directorate of Adult Education, 1982.

Ranjindoss, M.J.A., T. Ilanchezhian and K. Elumalai, *Total Literacy Campaign in Tamil Nadu: Status Report*. Madras: State Resource Centre for Non-formal Education, October 1932.

Saxena, J. C. and J.L. Sachdeva (eds.), *Adult Education: A People's Movement*. New Delhi: Proceedings of the Golden Jubilee Conference, May 22-25, 1989.

Unpublished Works

A. Muthumanickam, "A Study of Selected Rural Television Forums with Regard to knowledge and Attitude Levels of the Learners" (Unpublished Ph. D. thesis). University of Madras, 1993, p. 1.

INDEX